Bull from the Bush

Bull from the Bush

Australian Outback Yarns

Bob Flatt

First published in Australia in 1998 by
New Holland Publishers Pty Ltd
Sydney • Melbourne • London • Cape Town

3/2 Aquatic Drive, Frenchs Forest NSW 2086 Australia

167 Drummond Street, Carlton VIC 3053 Australia

24 Nutford Place, London, W1H 6DQ United Kingdom

80 McKenzie Street, Cape Town 8001 South Africa

Project Co-ordinator: Anna Sanders
Editor: Wendy Blaxland
Designer: Tricia McCallum
Printer: McPherson's Printing Group

National Library of Australia Cataloguing-in-Publication Data:

Flatt, Bob.
The bull from the bush: Australian outback yarns.

ISBN 1 86436 324 X

1. Flatt, Bob. 2. Jackeroos - Queensland - Biography. 3. Ranch life - Queensland. I. Strumfin, John. II. Title

636.201092

To Jimmy Mitchell and his wife, John Bennett, John Steele, Jack Ward, Boomarra Bill (I bet they are still rounding up your cattle from all around the Gulf), the cook's daughter, the Long brothers, Allen Milne, all the station managers and, last but by no means least, all the station and camp cooks then and now — without them life would have been unbearable.

The Gulf Country

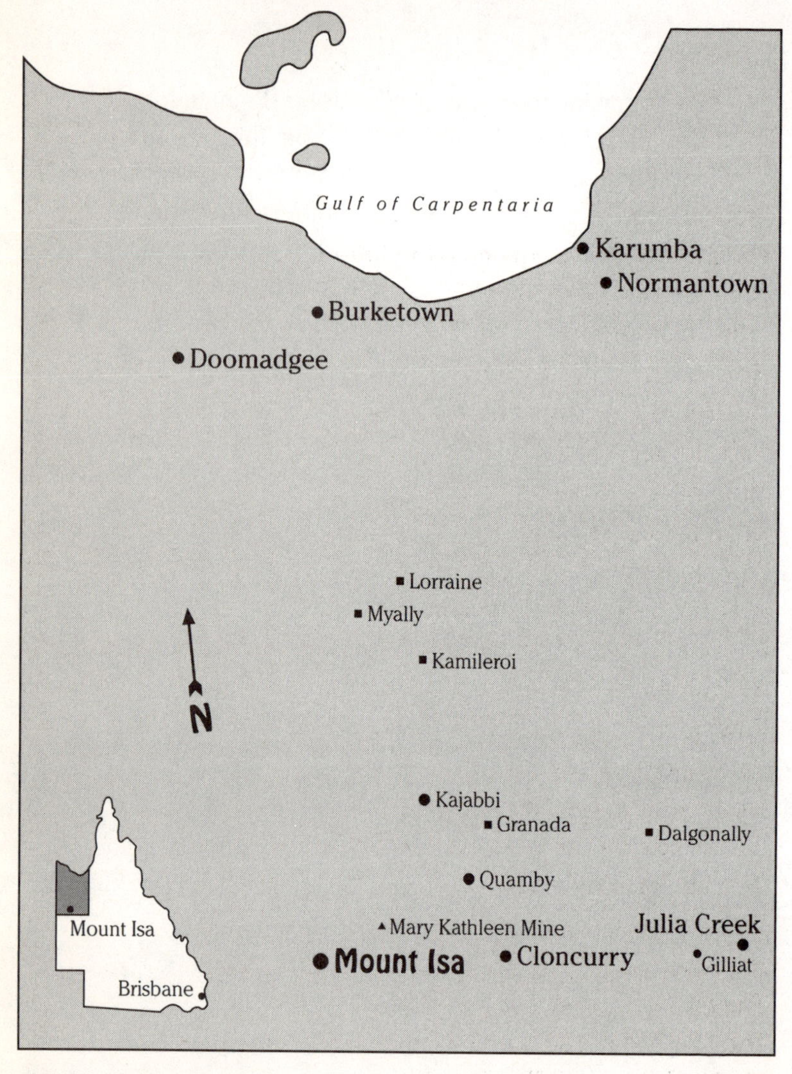

•Town ▪Homestead

Contents

Preface

Over the years I have been telling stories about my adventures in the outback of Australia or, to be more precise, the Gulf Country of northern Queensland. I first started my storytelling in 1959 as I headed for England on the New Zealand steamship *Rangitoto*. It helped pay my way.

While I was in England and Europe I told my bush stories to pub crowds in Kangaroo Valley and to hordes of people who were emigrating. Then, after I returned to Australia, many jobs later, I settled for a short time and opened a restaurant called Flatt's Cafe in the sleepy goldmining town of Sofala in New South Wales. The town had a population of about 50 people but Flatt's always had a crowd coming from near and far for the great tucker — and my yarns. Some of the stories are a bit shocking for city people, so remember that the outback people live a hard life, through drought and flood, and having animals die is an everyday occurrence.

Everyone wanted me to write a book about my adventures but until now I never seemed to be able to find the time. So to all my friends through the years, here's your copy of the bush tales. I hope they give you as much of a laugh in print as listening to them.

Regards and best wishes,

Bob Flatt

Bob (Captain Chaos)

The Sweet Smell of Cows in the Morning

In the swirling bulldust of the main cattle yard the ringers were pushing the cattle up to force them into the smaller drafting yards. It was my first time in the yards and I couldn't see a thing through the cloud of bulldust except the sun, which was like a huge red ball hanging over the yards, turning the dust cloud into a red haze.

'Bloody dust.'

I was in the dust, trying to push the mob of cattle through a gate. I couldn't see the opening or the cattle, there was dust in my eyes and ears, and my nose and mouth were covered with a cloth which was caked in the bloody stuff. My clothes were wet with sweat and my boots were covered in cow shit. I was feeling there had to be a better way to make a quid.

'Watch out for cattle coming back!' one of the ringers yelled over the noise of mooing cattle, the yells of the other ringers and the crack of stockwhips.

He had no sooner yelled the warning when out of the dust these huge bulky shapes with horns emerged heading straight for me. I couldn't run, I was in the middle of the yard and with my inattentiveness the cattle were upon me.

'Yeeeeeehhhhhhhh,' I yelled in panic at the top of my voice, at the same time waving my hands around like some demented lunatic. The first cow missed me with her horns but hit me with

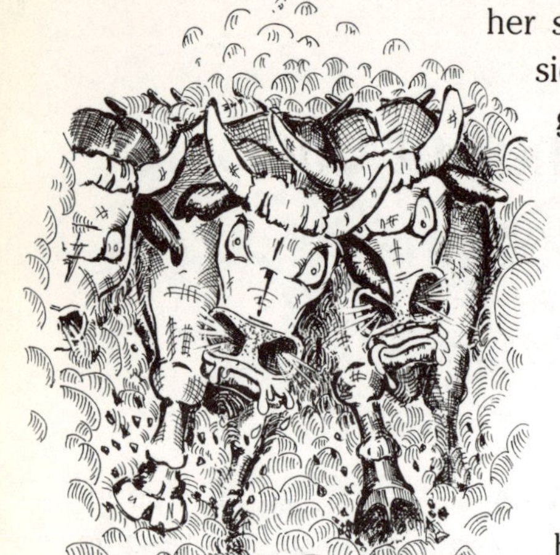

her shoulder and I spun into the side of another one. I tried to grab a hold to save myself but lost my footing and fell down into the urine and cow turds that were spread thickly through the ankle-deep bull-dust. As I sank into this mess I saw to my horror that another cow was about to hit me. I was lucky, the old girl baulked when she saw me, then leapt in the air, going right over me. I jumped to my feet, thinking how lucky I hadn't got horned . . .

'Bang! Crack!' As the cow landed she kicked back, hitting me in the ribs.

'Yeow!' I yelled as I went down for the second time. This time my ribs were on fire and the breath was knocked out of me. I lay in a heap trying to get air back in my lungs but all I seemed to be inhaling was dust.

'Hey! Get up, city slicker. You'll get trampled lying around resting there! Go and help in the other yard,' the head stockman said as he appeared, then disappeared into the dust cloud.

I could only croak a reply through the dust that was threatening to choke me.

I'm getting ahead of myself. I should explain how I, a city boy, got to be in a cattle yard in the Gulf Country of northern Queensland. So let's start at the beginning.

Outback and Beyond

I had all the good things in life up until the age of 15 — good schooling, good home — but I changed all that by leaving school, and through my godfather, Sid Eailes, who had properties in the western areas of New South Wales and knew the right people. He got me a job with Australian Estates in the Gulf Country. He said he didn't want me to be a jackaroo in New South Wales because most of them hung around the station homestead with the manager or owner and learnt nothing except doing the washing up and socialising. He had friends in Australian Estates and they had a cadet manager scheme which ran for three years, covering all aspects of station life. This included, much to my horror, a three year bookkeeping course by correspondence. Sid made a deal with them — he sold them his New South Wales properties and became the Sydney manager for Australian Estates.

My deal was I could have a job for life as long as I got through the first 12 month probation period, which I did. I then went on and became the youngest cadet Australian Estates had ever taken on. They normally took boys who had finished Agricultural College at about 18 or 19 years old.

I had improved my riding during the holidays by working at Judy Vockler's Challis Riding Stables near Centennial Park in Sydney. My job was to clean out the stables and ride and exercise some of the horses boarding there. Judy was a no-nonsense disciplinarian and a fine horsewoman, and I had a teenage crush on her because she was very beautiful. I was so helpful Judy offered me a full-time job, but she was married to a huge bloke so I thought I would only get into trouble if I made my feelings known. And I was only a daydreaming kid of 15 and she was an older woman in her 20s, married, and with a very busy social life. Twenty years later when I bumped into her in Sofala, she remembered a Bob but it took about half an hour to convince her that it was me. So much for the impression I made as a would-be admirer.

The trip to the north from Sydney took nearly a week. Mother had packed just about everything except the kitchen sink. I had a huge suitcase full of ties — maybe 50 of them — and lots of handkerchiefs (I lugged this heavy bag around and to the best of my knowledge I never opened it), plus the things the company asked me to buy: a diary, riding boots (I bought flat-heeled Baxters), jodhpurs, shirts with button-down pockets, a pocketknife, a broad-brimmed hat and a swag. This was a rectangle of canvas with a pocket at one end in which to put your clothes and belongings; then you would roll it up with your blankets inside and secure it with two leather belts.

At Central Station, bustling, noisy, crowded and full of steam, surrounded by all my luggage, I said my goodbyes to my mother and father. It was a tearful parting because I was to stay away for two years before the company paid my fare back.

With a rush I was on the train and off to Brisbane. The trip was full of excitement, and I had great fun throwing toilet paper out to all the fettlers and railway gangs that yelled out for paper — they were wanting newspapers or magazines to read. Along the way there were enamel signs for Billy Tea, Griffiths Bros and King's Kidney Pills, telling the passengers how many miles it was to go before they could buy them.

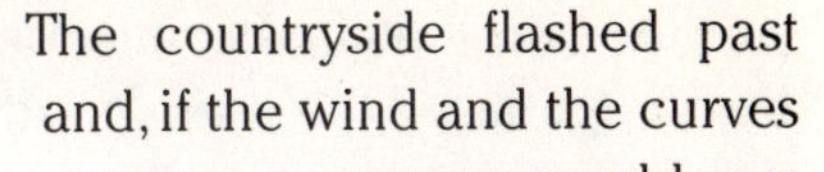

The countryside flashed past and, if the wind and the curves were wrong, we would cop coal dust and ash in the window, so after a while everyone was filthy. Arriving in Brisbane was exciting but after carrying the bags up the hill to the People's Palace (a temperance hotel) I was bushed.

I went out that evening, walking around like a world traveller, but inside I was wondering if I had done the right thing, leaving all my mates behind in Sydney. Back on the train, I met Allen Jones, who was older than me and had just finished Gatton Agricultural College. He talked about how hard it would be for me, being so young and knowing nothing about animal husbandry. I nearly got into a fight with him but I kept my peace.

The trip up to Townsville took two days and I was glad to get off the train and have a shower. The hotel we stayed in had a bar and I had enough money to get drunk, thanks to the company which had advanced me travel money. The next day we boarded the Inlander, a new streamlined train, to take us to Julia Creek. Looking out the huge picture windows at the countryside racing by, I felt self-doubt creeping back into my mind. Would I be all right, or would I fail and have to return to Sydney with my tail between my legs?

The country was flat, with short stunted trees that looked olive green in the harsh sunlight — and was that sun strong! You could feel its heat through the tinted glass of the window.

'Next stop Julia Creek, Julia Creek in five minutes — we stop for five minutes,' the train guard yelled as he passed through our car.

I looked out the window at the flat landscape and couldn't see a town anywhere in sight. We grabbed our bags and made our way to the exit door. I went to get off on the left hand side but the guard told us there was only one track and the town was on the right, so we could alight on that side.

The train came to a halt and the guard threw the doors open. A blast of hot air hit us — no, not hot, more like a furnace — and it smelt of animals.

We followed the lead of the people in front and threw our bags out on to the ground. I stepped down and as my foot went into the ground I was up to my ankles in the red dust which rose around Allen and me. Through the dust appeared a slim, medium-built bloke, calling out our names. It turned out to be the manager of Dalgonally Station, Neil. I tried to brush the dust off but that just made things worse. I was sweating in the hot sun, wearing the sports coat and woollen tie that Mother had packed.

'We won't go out until the late afternoon, it will be cooler then. I think we'll retire to the pub until then, okay?' the manager said with a smile.

We threw our gear into the ute and made our way down the street to the pub. Julia Creek — what a town! It had wooden walkways and the pub had batwing doors. I was in my element — cowboy land. I started to feel better and after a few beers I felt I could take on an army. We sat around telling the manager about ourselves. I noticed that the stockmen in the bar were drinking nips of OP rum with beer chasers. All wore Cuban heels (high-heeled boots), some with huge spurs. Most wore moleskin trousers that were tight on the leg and shirts with long sleeves and button-down pockets.

Around their waist they wore an extra leather belt that had nothing to do with holding up their pants. On this belt were threaded leather pouches to hold a watch, a tin of wax matches, an all-purpose pocketknife and two cutting knives. They were all wearing leather leggings. I asked the manager about this and he told me that when you are riding in the Channel Country the grass stalks come between the saddle and your legs. That causes the seeds to rub off through your pants and into your skin and if your legs aren't looked after they become infected.

I looked at myself in my flat-heeled Baxters, woollen tie, sports coat and wide brown pants . . . I didn't have to tell anybody that I was new here and from the city.

We left the hotel at around six o'clock when it was still light. Allen and I sat in the back of the ute. There was a lot to see — kangaroos, emus and hundreds of parrots. The country was flat with some rocky outcrops, the thick dust was red and although we had tied handkerchiefs over our faces, the dust seeped into our ears, noses and mouths, so we had to spit every so often to clear our throats. We took it in turns to open the gates — I think there were around 18 on that road at the time. By the time we got to the station I had learnt to open nearly all types of gates, from those made from fencing wire and wooden poles to the ones made from pipe and netting.

At first sight as we came through the house paddock the station looked like a small village. In front of us was the main homestead surrounded by gardens, and behind that was the kitchen and dining room. Out on its own was the meat house, then the horse yards and sheds. The jackaroos' quarters were next to the gardens of the main house, next were the married quarters and the ringers' or stockmen's quarters, and behind that the quarters for the Aborigines.

We were shown to our rooms and told to go up to the

kitchen, where the cook would give us something to eat, and then we should hit the sack. We would meet everyone in the morning as they were already in their quarters. But before we went to bed we were told that as trainee managers there were a few rules to be learnt: we were to stay away from the ringers' quarters and on no account go anywhere near the Aboriginal quarters; leave the house girls alone, and not hang around the married women. I don't remember much else about that night, as I was so tired.

Before dawn the first bell rang to tell us to get up and have a wash, as breakfast would be ready in half an hour. When we arrived at the dining room on the second bell both Allen and I were called over to the head of the table by a bloke sitting there. He turned out to be Jim Mitchell, a thickset, muscled, dark-haired bloke. You knew from the start that he wouldn't stand any funny business.

We introduced ourselves and sat down for breakfast.

Most of the talk was about the stock and the muster that was coming up, so I ate and listened. Just a small note here. Swearing was second nature to all these blokes. I haven't used it much in writing the dialogue but if I did a simple sentence would go something like this:

'Open the f . . . ing gate and let the bloody horses out you f . . . ing idiot, before the f . . . ing things get f . . . ing hurt.' I must admit that Mother wasn't impressed when I came home on a visit after two years of learning this language, plus finishing every sentence with 'ay'.

'I haven't got your horses in, so I'll find you something to do around the homestead for a few days,' said Jim. 'Can you ride?'

'Yes, of course I can,' I answered without thinking.

'Good. We'll see at the end of the week.' Jim and the rest of the ringers laughed.

I went back to my room and surprised a young pretty

Aboriginal girl about the same age as myself making the beds and cleaning, I tried to make friends but I could see she was scared.

I was confronted by the head girl and told in no uncertain words to get out and not to talk to the staff. I didn't tell her that it was the first time in my life I had talked to a black person and that I was curious as I had heard so much about them.

In later months I was able to speak to the pretty girl in my room when she was cleaning. She only trusted me enough to talk to me in the beginning, but after I had been there six months we used to hold hands and steal a kiss in the darkness of the gardens. The only time she stayed clear of me was when I was able to get some illegal OP rum and get drunk. Then she was gone, slipping away like a black shadow — she told me the mission warned girls about white men and drink. She became pregnant to one of the black ringers and was sent back to the mission to have the baby. I didn't see her again.

My days working around the station got rid of a lot of city fat and my hands hardened up after the blisters broke, since they had me chopping wood, digging holes and repairing fences.

There was something that I will always remember. After breakfast I would go down to the horse yards and watch old Charlie. Old Charlie was retired on the station. In his younger days he had been a jockey, so he was short and bandy-legged. On Dalgonally Old Charlie's job — before he got too old and a tractor was used to replace him — was cleaning out the bore drains. I should explain. The artesian bores sunk into the artesian basin flowed very hot out of huge pipes into trenches that then carried the water for miles. Some trenches were 20 miles long. With six huge draft horses in harness Charlie would drag a plough-like device clearing these trenches. (One of the worst jobs I can remember in my first days at the station was having to cut the prickly bushes away so the cattle could get in to drink and maintenance could be carried out on the drain.)

Every morning the horses would come in from the horse paddock — there were around 50 of them. They would come into the big yard all milling and pushing, and Charlie would climb through the rails and stand to one side. Then he would call his horses by name and they would come out of the mob and stand in pairs as if they were in harness. Charlie would yell for the ringers to open the gate and he would call to the horses and they would walk out as if they were in harness. He would direct them to a shady spot and while they stood in formation he would groom them and clean their hooves. This little man fussing over these huge animals that he loved, it was a great sight, one that I was privileged to see before it disappeared forever.

The days rolled on. I worked during the day and talked about city life at night. It was at this early time the ringers nicknamed me Doc (after a Labor politician called Doc Evatt because I was always arguing about everything). They would ask me where I got the information from (like what book or what newspaper) and if I couldn't tell them, they would say they didn't believe me. That used to shut me up for a while, but not for long.

It was at this time that I learnt to kill and dress the meat for the station. We ran what we called 'killers' in the horse paddock. These killers were cattle that had been picked because they were well-covered but were no good to breed from. About once a fortnight the cowboy (the station hand who works around the main homestead doing all the jobs like watering the gardens, helping the cook, milking and feeding the pigs) would bring the killer in and yard it. Then when the ringers arrived back from mustering in the afternoon one of them would come over to the killing yards and shoot it.

The first few times were the hardest for me. To watch someone kill an animal and let it bleed in cold blood, showing no emotion, was very tough for a city boy. After the killing the beast was butchered and the best fresh meat carried to the meat house to hang and set overnight. The rest was corned in the corning trough by rubbing coarse salt and saltpetre into cuts made across the grain of the meat so that it cured all the way through. The next day my first job was to take the fresh meat from the meat house, give it to the cook and help him pack it into the kero fridges.

In the first days of my new life I learnt how to fence, sharpen butcher's knives, cut up meat, drive tractors, garden, live in quarters with other blokes, make a bridle and keep out of sight of the manager because whenever he saw you he'd give you another job.

In the Dust Again

'Doc, you're coming out with me tomorrow, so be ready to go straight after breakfast, okay?' Jim said at the dinner table after I had been on Dalgonally for about two months. I had only ridden the old horses in the night paddock, so I was excited, but at the same time a bit apprehensive about what sort of horse they would give me. I had heard a lot of worrying stories about the horses that the ringers gave the new chums.

The next morning saw me down at the yards as they drafted out the horses each ringer was to ride that day.

As the horses were drafted through the yards, the ones the ringers wanted to ride were stopped in the round catching yard and each ringer would duck under the rails, or climb the gate, to select and catch the horse of his choice, then lead it out into a bigger yard to saddle up.

My turn came and I stepped into the round yard, walked slowly up to my horse's head and tried to put the bridle on. The big bay gelding knew that I wasn't sure of myself and kept turning away.

'Don't walk behind him,' yelled Jim.

Too late! Bang! The horse hit me with both back legs and I flew across the yard into the rails.

'Come on, we haven't got all day to catch him.'

I staggered up and shakily limped around the yard, staying

well clear of his hindquarters. Try as I might, I couldn't get the bloody bridle on his head. When I approached him with my hand out to touch his face, he would throw his head up in the air and start to swing around and I would jump back because I didn't want to be kicked again.

The next thing, Jim was in the yard at my side.

'Look, I'll show you once, so watch me. Put the top strap of your bridle in your left hand with your reins over them, put out your right hand and walk up to the horse's shoulder and put your hand on his neck, like this. (Whoa boy, steady up.) Hold on to the mane, talk to him. (Steady boy, stand still.) Then slip the reins around his neck, hold him steady with them, then slip the bridle up over his head. You might have to move your rein hand to get hold of the top of the bridle and make him open his mouth for the bit. Then do up the throat strap and lead him out.'

Jim said all this as he caught the bay and put the bridle on for me. I led the horse out to the large yard where the other stockmen were saddling up.

One of the older ringers came up with a saddle and saddle blanket over his arm.

'This one's the best of a bad lot. As you can see, its got a high back so you shouldn't fall out backwards and the knee pads are around five inches high so the only thing that should get you out of this saddle is starvation.'

I led my horse over to the rail and put the saddle blanket on him, then the stock saddle, but I hit his flank with a stirrup and he shied and pulled away. I dropped the saddle in the dust as I tried to stop him. That only made matters worse as I tripped over the saddle and fell to the ground.

'When you've finished f . . . ing about get that saddle off the ground — and don't let me see you misusing station property again,' Jim was standing over me bellowing. This was when I first realised that if, in these Gulf Country stations, you made a blue, the gear seemed to be more important than yourself.

'Look, you've been used to quiet horses, so I'll show you the best way to put the saddle on,' he said as he picked it up off the ground.

'It's better to not tie the horse up but to hold the reins so you can keep him close to you. I find that putting the offside stirrup, the girth and the surcingle over the saddle helps. You lift and slide the saddle on to his back like this, then you walk around the horse and take the stirrup, girth and surcingle off the top of the saddle.' He was talking as he performed all these actions, with me following him.

'Then you come back to the near side and lean underneath and fasten them up tight. You'll notice that the cord surcingle has a red hide strap, the strap goes up through the ring and is laced up. This is the main piece that holds the saddle on, so get it right and tight or you'll be thrown, saddle and all.'

It all looked terribly complicated to me.

'The leather girth is mainly used for breastplates and is secondary to the cord surcingle. The cords let the skin breathe and the sweat out. This stops the horse chafing behind the legs, which causes sores.' With those words he was finished saddling up for me.

It was time to mount. I put my hand over the saddle and grabbed the monkey or jug handle (a strap fitted to the offside top of the saddle and used to help you get mounted fast — if the horse pigroots you can hold on to this to stop yourself coming off) and slowly started to pull myself aboard.

Bang crash whoooooosh!

I was too slow and hadn't reined the horse's head around, so he was able to run past me — and to make matters worse he cow-kicked me in the stomach as he went by, so I fell to the ground. This wasn't a good way to show I could ride.

I got up, dusted myself off, then limped over and caught the horse. This time I did it right. I was in the saddle quickly and ready for anything. I trotted him around the yard without any trouble. Then it was time to go out of the yard into the horse paddock.

'Don't just walk him, canter him around a bit,' the head stockman yelled.

I kicked him into a canter. Then as we cantered down the paddock I thought I would turn him, so I pulled sharply on the rein, just as I would have done in Sydney. He turned …

Oh no, where's the horse?

I was airborne! He'd turned so fast I'd had no chance to turn with him. The horse was an old hand at this and he was back underneath me before I hit the ground. He did this a number of times. It must have looked funny, with me going out one way and the horse trying to catch me. It wasn't long before the horse — even with all his skills — couldn't save me. I hit the dirt with a crash that knocked the wind out of me. One of the ringers chased after the horse and caught it. As I sat in the swirling dust I started to have second thoughts about the life of a stockman.

'What sort of horses did you ride before?' asked the ringer. 'You were so heavy-handed I thought you were driving a truck.' I hadn't ridden any horses with good mouths that could turn on a tuppeny piece. All the hard-mouthed hacks I had ridden needed a lot of strength to turn them.

In the first six months I came off at least once a day. I had a habit of pulling my glasses off whenever I thought a horse was going to drop me, because I thought the glasses might break on my face and blind me. Bishops, the optometrists in Sydney, loved me. There was always a broken pair of glasses on the way down, a pair being fixed and at least two pairs back with me in camp.

I was a very stiff and sore trainee when I arrived at breakfast the next day to face another day of riding and mustering. Over the next few days the hair on the inside of my legs got rubbed off and the skin was rubbed raw, so they gave me a bottle of metho to rub on, to strengthen the skin. From that day on, if I haven't been riding for some time I've always shaved the inside of my legs and rubbed metho on them to stop them from getting sore. Some of the blokes wore pantyhose for the first few days, and did we give them hell!

Horses Can't Fly, Can They?

For months after arriving on Dalgonally I wasn't taken out to the mustering camp, but when there were cattle to be moved, they'd let me help. I was always told to stay where I was put and the only place I was allowed to be on a drive was at the tail end of the mob, with the boys. This meant I ate dust all day, it was hot, and there were clouds of flies attracted to the smell of cattle, as the smell of urine and shit was high.

To drive cattle you started out with one ringer riding in front of the mob. His job was to slow down the few cattle that wanted to rush off from the mob and at the same time to show the mob the way. There were a couple of riders down each side of the mob, on the wings, to stop any cattle escaping from the sides. The rest of the ringers, Aborigines and learners were behind on the tail, making the slow and weak beasts keep up. These drives were short, a day at the most from yards to holding paddocks, or from where the cattle had been mustered into yards. After yarding they could be drafted and the sale stock would then be driven back to a paddock near the station so the buyers could come out and look them over.

I was called in early afternoon to stop fixing the horse yard, saddle up, ride out and help the ringers, who had been mustering all morning and were bringing in a large mob. I was to meet them and help bring the mob through the gidgee scrub to the yards. The horse tailer had yarded up a very leggy ex-racehorse for me to ride and as we rode out of the yards Jim told me to keep a tight rein on him because he was a bit headstrong. I said I would, not quite knowing what Jim meant. It was pretty hot and I wasn't looking forward to eating dust all afternoon. We rode down out of the hills from the camp and across the black soil plain to the dust and the black specks that were moving towards us.

When we rode up I was sent to — you guessed it — the tail to help the boys at the back. They were very pleased to see me because with me as an extra hand there were just enough of them to be able to take a break, one at a time. The break consisted of riding out of the dust cloud to a bit of shade, having a smoke that didn't taste like dust and clearing your clogged-up nose and choked-up throat and lungs. I had been working the tail for a couple of hours and my whip arm felt as if it was falling off, when out of the haze came Jim.

'Hey, Doc, they'll be right on the tail. Come out on the wing with me for a while.'

I didn't need any forcing. I reined the old horse in and joined him.

It was easier on the wing. The cattle were following the leaders and only one or two of them would make a break for freedom.

Jim showed me how to cope when a beast ran out — you kicked your horse out and kept wide until you were abreast of him, then cracked your whip and yelled out. If the beast didn't turn, you turned your horse in onto the animal's shoulder and forced it to join the mob again with a crack of the whip. Back the beast would go. It seemed so easy that I couldn't wait to have a go.

The mob was approaching the gidgee trees when a monster bullock decided to make a run for it.

Jim yelled, 'Go for it, Doc!'

I gathered the old racehorse in and the next thing we were flying over the ground faster than I had ever ridden before — the horse was stretched out, trying to go faster. We crossed the grass country at a great rate of knots, catching up to the galloping bullock. We were approaching the bullock from the rear which meant it was trying to gallop faster to get away from us. I realised the old galloper had the bit between his teeth and there was nothing I could do, I couldn't turn him or stop him. The only thing I could do was to stay on the bastard's back. We charged up beside the bullock and my horse put his shoulder into its neck and started to push. Nothing happened. We were galloping alongside the bullock and getting nowhere. I couldn't hear anything, except the pounding of hooves and the heavy breathing of the two animals.

I took a quick look ahead.

Oh no!

There was a large stand of gidgee trees right in front of us and the bullock had set his sights on this scrub. I pulled frantically on the reins so the horse would turn away from the bullock. Nothing was happening. The horse had the bit firmly between his teeth and no matter how hard I pulled him, he kept leaning against the bullock's neck. I was panic-stricken because the trees were coming up on us at a million miles an hour. I kept wrestling with the bit and suddenly we were only about 20 feet away and I could see a break between two trees. It was only large enough for one of us to go through at a time and the bullock had made up his mind that it was going to be him. I yelled out as the tree came up.

'Jesus!!!'

Crash!! Snap! Snap! Bang!

We hit at full gallop. The tree was angled away from us so the horse and I shot up the trunk. The bloody bullock had gone through the opening. We must have gone two horse lengths up into the tree before we stopped. Then the horse slowly started to topple backwards towards the ground. I grabbed hold of a branch to stop myself falling under him as he slid down to the ground with a crash, where he lay on his back, tossing around and snorting.

Suddenly Jim was pulling his horse up underneath me, yelling, 'Don't bloody well hang up in that bloody tree while a good station saddle is getting f . . . ed. Get down and get that bloody saddle off. If it's broken, you'll pay to get it fixed.'

I was hanging up in the tree, looking around in shock, wondering if I had broken anything.

'Don't hang around all bloody day, do it now.'

I dropped from the tree and got the saddle off the horse, who by this time was standing shakily on his legs, looking as bewildered as me.

'Walk him around a bit and then saddle him up and catch up with us.'

With that he turned and galloped off. I walked myself around, making sure I was all right. When I got the courage to get back on, the old horse was a bit shocked, and he didn't want to canter for the rest of the afternoon.

These Queensland stockmen didn't give a bugger about you unless you were near death — they worried more about the horses and the gear.

I've Heard of Loaves and Fishes

One of the first jobs on Dalgonally, not counting the post hole digging and fencing, was killing. As the station killed its own cattle for meat, one of the jobs for the ringers left around the station was to saddle up, ride out to a paddock close to the homestead, pick out a few cattle that looked in good condition and walk them towards a clump of trees, where a rifleman sat up a tree and waited until the cattle were beneath. He would then pick out the one in the best condition and shoot it. As the animal hit the ground the riders would move the rest of the cattle away. One of the men in the truck would rush in with a knife and cut the throat of the animal so that it bled well. If this wasn't done straight away the meat would be inedible.

If there weren't any trees around, we would move the cattle as close to the truck or Landrover as we could and keep out of the line of fire because sometimes there were near misses — not all stockmen are good shots. So that the cattle were easy to manage and to minimise the risk of the meat getting tainted, we would always kill in a different spot.

One particular day the head stockman, Jim Mitchell, and I had been sent out early to muster some fat cows and walk them in towards the station, as we had a visitor from head office in Melbourne. He had brought his guns with him and wanted to shoot something.

These fat cows had been spayed because they were no longer good for breeding. After that they grew enormous. The ones we were sent for were waiting to go to market, so they were huge.

As we rode out Jim kept saying to me over and over, 'Look out for this city bloke with his high-powered rifle. He could hit any of us if we get in his line of vision.'

We found the cows by the waterhole. They had just started to move out to feed, so we had no trouble moving eight of them towards the spot about a mile away where we were to meet the Landrover with the top shot from the city aboard.

We arrived at the spot early and the cattle settled down to graze. We sat on our horses talking, or rather me talking and Jim listening as I was still a city boy and couldn't stand silence.

In the distance we could see the dust as the Landrover approached.

'Ride down and tell them to stop on that rise there,' Jim said, pointing. 'You stay down by the vehicle out of the way and I'll walk them down to you.'

I trotted down to where they had stopped and waited to see where he wanted them to station themselves.

The Landrover had its back canvas off and the windscreen down on the bonnet. Sitting in the front was the manager and next to him was the bloke from the city, holding this huge rifle with the biggest telescopic sight I had ever seen. By the look of the gun, I thought it would stop an elephant. I noticed that he looked very excited and that's not good when a person's handling a gun. In the back sat one of the station's black roustabouts and you could see that he agreed with me, he did not look happy. In the back with him were all the knives and feed bags to lay the meat out on when we loaded it. I dismounted and walked down behind the Rover. They stopped and waited while Jim brought the cows up close to us.

I could hear the manager asking the city bloke, 'Do you want to shoot over the bonnet, or get out and shoot?'

'No, I'm all right here. I don't want to get too close to those brutes, they're huge. I feel safer in here,' he answered as he cocked the bloody thing.

Jim had moved the cattle to where we had planned to butcher them. He started yelling for the bloke to shoot. Then suddenly, all hell broke loose.

Boooooooooooommmmmmmmmm! The cannon went off, deafening us all. This was followed by a loud metallic ring and the buzz as the bullet ricocheted between the two of us standing at the back. Then — sssssssssss — the sound of escaping air.

We threw ourselves on the ground.

'Whoa, you bastard,' I yelled as I was dragged through the dust by my horse, who had taken fright and was trying to get away. I got my feet under me and regained control of my horse. By the time I walked back, I could hear the city bloke apologising for shooting the spare tyre.

Straight away I could see what had happened. While he was aiming through the telescopic sights he could see the cow, but the barrel of the rifle was lower and up against the spare wheel which was fixed to the bonnet. When he pulled the trigger, he shot the spare wheel point blank — and by the look of the hole, it was stone dead! The bullet had gone in through the rubber, ricocheted off the metal rim and come back between the two of them in the front and past us in the back.

Suddenly Jim's voice penetrated my ringing ears. 'Doc, stop bloody daydreaming and get yourself up here and give me a bloody hand.'

When I looked in his direction I could see Jim was having trouble stopping the frightened cows taking off in every direction to escape the noise.

I swung into the saddle and galloped over to give him a hand.

'These cattle should be let go,' Jim yelled to the manager. 'They're getting too excited and hot, and the meat won't be any good.'

'One more shot,' the manager yelled back.

Bbbbbooooooooooommmmmmmm! The cannon went off again. One of the cows went down and as I cantered in to get the knives the cow behind her also collapsed in a heap.

'Christ, the stupid bastard's shot has gone right through the first cow and hit the second bastard. Jesus, look at all that meat!'

On the ground were two very large, dead cows. When butchered there would be nearly a couple of tons of meat.

Jim and I tied up our horses, walked over and started to cut up the meat. The city bloke was all apologies, which didn't impress us at all.

We had to put the canvas cover back on the Rover to hold all the meat. We were cutting and trying to stack the hot, wet, slippery meat into the back of the Rover, and with a lot of cursing and swearing we managed to fill the back and lace it closed. But that wasn't the end, there were tons more. So we started to pack it in on top of the meat in the back from over the front seats. A few hours later, with the ringer and the city bloke riding on the bonnet, the overloaded vehicle headed for the station, while Jim and I rode back in comfort on our horses.

'Now you can see what I was talking about when we were riding out, those city blokes can't be trusted with guns.'

When we got back we unsaddled and let our horses go. Then

we made our way to the meat house where most of the ringers had gathered. As we approached, one of them came over to us.

'What's going on? What are we going to do with all this bloody meat? There's mountains of the bloody stuff and we can only pack away three days' worth of fresh meat in the kero fridges. What the hell are we going to do with the rest?'

'Salt it down.' Jimmy held up his hand as every ringer started to swear. 'It's the only thing to do with it, we can't waste it.' There was a groan from the ringers. 'I know it means we'll be eating corned beef for over a month but there's nothing else we can do.'

With groans and a lot of swearing the ringers went back to scarfing the meat and rubbing salt and saltpetre into it. The salted meat filled the meat house to overflowing, so the dogs ate well and the ringers, knowing what was in store for them, ate as much of the fresh meat as they could fit in so more could be stored in the fridges.

I didn't know what a month's diet of salted meat was like before this. The cook was great, cooking it in every way he could dream up. After that month was over I could have written a salted meat cookery book. To name just a few of the main courses that month, we had Burdekin duck (slabs of corned beef fried in batter), cottage pie (slabs of corned beef minced and covered with mashed potato), corned beef for lunch (slabs of corned beef with yellow pickles in damper), boiled corned beef with vegetables (slabs of corned beef boiled in four gallon tins with carrots, onions and potatoes), and savoury mince (slabs of corned beef minced with carrots, onions and lots of tomato sauce). The reason for the 'slabs' was to get rid of the corned beef as quickly as possible.

Even the dogs had turned their noses up. No matter how we tried, it still took four weeks to get rid of it all and if the bloody city bloke had stayed around, the ringers would have shot him!

An Untimely Mudbath

Horses are the most unpredictable of animals and when I was out for the first time on mustering camp at Dalgonally I learnt a lot about their odd ways.

In my first few days I was subjected to horses that were quiet to ride and slow to take off, but they were old and crafty.

We saddled up early one morning in the cold and dark, around five o'clock because we had a long way to ride before starting to muster the cattle back towards the long waterhole near our camp.

After the morning rodeo of the ringers getting their fresh mounts under control, we set out with Jim, the head stockman, in the lead, then the ringers two abreast behind him, followed by us jackaroos and then the Aborigines.

We rode over to the waterhole and started to follow the shoreline around, as we were going to muster on the other side, when Jim called out that we were going to wade across to save us an hour or so. The ringers started to complain that they didn't want to muster in wet clothes all day. To ease their worries Jim sent one of the ringers across on the understanding that he could go back to camp and change if it became too deep.

The ringer rode his horse into the water and started to wade out. The waterhole was around 150 yards wide and quite a number of miles long. The water was a sickly pale grey tinged with green, so you wouldn't want to get covered in the stuff. The ringer was about halfway across and was holding his legs up to save getting wet but the horse was finding it heavy going and the ringer called back that the mud was about three feet deep and the water only a foot deep.

He made it across and waved okay. Jim led us into the water in single file as there could have been holes on either side of where the first ringer had crossed. We got spread out, some of the horses refused to go into the murky water and pigrooted around until their riders got them into the water. I was in the lagoon, making my way slowly across. Jim and the lead riders were over. They were sitting on the their horses watching the rest of us come slowly across, having to listen to Jim yell for us to hurry it up because it was getting light and we had a long way to go.

Suddenly my horse stopped. I kicked him but it didn't make the least bit of difference. The riders around me started to shout and hit him to get him going. I kicked and hit him with my feet, my reins and my fists but it didn't seem to make the slightest bit of difference to him. The horse started to lean to the right. Everyone was calling out that he was going to roll. I was bellowing and scrambling around on his back like a demented circus rider. As he knelt down I was almost standing in the saddle and as he rolled I was still trying to keep on top. I could hear voices telling me not to let go of the reins but that was the least of my worries — I was trying to keep out of the foul-smelling, evil-looking water that was rising around me.

I think I was standing on the saddle flap when I lost my balance. With a strangled cry — or was it a scream? — my feet went from under me and I hit the water. Water? That was only a foot deep. It was the mud I went down into and for a few seconds, while I fought to get to the surface, I was very worried. But I finally emerged, to the cheers of the ringers and the curses of the head stockman. Of course, I hadn't held onto my reins so the horse was up and leapfrogging to the bank on the camp side, leaving me standing looking like a grey mud statue, wondering how I was going to get my feet out of the mud with my boots on since I didn't fancy holding my breath and trying to locate the boots under three feet of mud.

Jim told me — no, he yelled at me — that if I had worn bloody spurs this would never have bloody happened. And what's more, I was to go back to camp, get the night horse, ride out and catch my horse, clean the saddle and wait at the camp. I could help the cook and when the men came in to change horses for yarding up I could help with that too.

All this took place as I stood up to my waist in the middle of the lagoon, covered in mud and wondering if I could get my feet out. One of the boys rode in and told me to grab his stirrup so he could pull me out of the mud. I grabbed the iron and he kicked his horse out. At first I thought that I was going to be pulled in half and just when I thought that I would have to let go, I came free with a loud sucking noise. But my boots stayed and I was lying spread flat out in the water in my socks. I had to let go of the stirrup and swim and crawl through the foot of water to the bank.

It took me some time to reach the shore and when I did I felt as if I had broken my ankles. Now barefoot, since somewhere on my way to shore my socks had disappeared, I was not looking forward to the walk back to camp, because I thought of what could lurk in the grass like snakes, scorpions and the dreaded burr. As I made my way cautiously through the grass I realised that I had lost my huge flat-heeled Baxters and didn't have any other riding boots. I was so mad I thought of all the ways that I could murder my horse but that all fell away when I caught sight of him, with his reins caught up on a dead branch. So I didn't have to walk home after all. I rode back to the camp with my toes gripping the stirrups. I must have looked a sight to the cook as I rode up, this barefoot apparition covered from head to foot in grey mud. It took a few hours to clean myself and the gear.

That night around the fire I was sold my first pair of R M Williams Cuban-heeled boots that one of the ringers had sent away for. The boots were too tight for him but they fitted me like a glove. The ringers pulled out an R M Williams catalogue and when I got back to the station I sent away for moleskin trousers and a new hat (I was still wearing jodhpurs and a flat-brimmed sheep grazier's hat).

I could roll the brim up on both sides of my new Stetson and, after that I swapped the little stubby city spurs which went with the flat-heeled boots and got myself a goose-necked pair that spun when I walked, I looked like a real stockman. But I only got to wear those spurs once in Jim Mitchell's camp. Most bush horses never needed to be spurred on like Arabs, Australian stock ponies and quarter horses. Good head stockmen would not allow you to wear them on most of the horses but when horses were tired at the end of a muster and there was no change of horses for yarding up we were allowed to wear them. A lot of the top riders wore them but they only used them to keep their horses out of trouble when they were tired. For example, if a bull turned and charged you when you were yarding up and your horse was tired, you hit your horse with the spurs and since he wasn't used to them he would jump, saving both of you from getting hurt.

The indiscriminate use of spurs on good or quiet horses would have you thrown out of the mustering camp on your ear and you wouldn't find a job in the Gulf or, for that matter, anywhere else in Australia. I witnessed a lot of fights over too free a use of spurs by ringers who saw horses as coming first.

Slipping the Slipper In

It was at this camp that I witnessed another amazing scene, one that would alter my treatment of horses.

When we were mustering near someone else's property we always let them know so that they would send a few ringers over to help with the muster and take home any of their own cattle that had roamed onto our land.

We always had a great time in the mustering camp, as these stockmen would bring with them their buckjumpers, cutting-out horses and anything they had made to sell like rope halters, greenhide ropes, bridles, belts and whips. It was a party with no grog or women — but with storytelling about the musters, the great rides and the last trip to town.

Into the camp one afternoon rode three men with 16 horses, two with pack saddles. The stockman in the lead was very popular and everyone in our camp, including Jim, went out to meet him.

I looked him over. He was medium built, middle-aged, running a little to fat. To my amazement he also had a riding boot on the right foot and a checked woollen slipper on the left. I found out later that he had gout and couldn't get a riding boot on. The horse only had a halter, without a bit, and the rider didn't seem to be directing him. I was fascinated. Here was a man who loved horses and was classed as one of the best riders in that part of Queensland. I followed him around, asking questions, until Jim told me to give him a break.

The next morning was quite a sight. As we got ready to go out mustering, everyone was showing off. Horses were pigrooting everywhere and our top riders were saddling up the buckjumping horses from the other station. It was a great hour before Jim called a halt to the fun.

During the muster that day I witnessed some top riding by both camps but it was in the afternoon at my first cattle draft that my eyes were opened.

We had about 1200 head of cattle. We let them calm down and held them in a camp with lots of flat ground around them. All the riders went into the horse yards to change horses. This was it, the time when riders and horses become one.

I still didn't quite know what was going on. I knew that we would hold the cattle in the camp and two of the best riders and their cutting-out horses would go into the mob to cut out the cows and calves that were strangers without disturbing the cattle. They would also cut out any cattle of our own that we wanted to separate from the mob before yarding, because once in the yards the cows with calves could not be drafted as they wouldn't be together.

The bloke from the place next door came out with a smallish chestnut mare with no bridle for me to ride. I was told that it would turn on a sixpence, so to be careful. Jim and most of the Dalgonally camp had Arabs because the station used to breed remounts for the army and it was proud of its Arab-stockhorse cross. They were beautiful horses, horses that would go until they fell over from exhaustion. Even after a big day they would be prancing around when we were yarding up. Some of them were still working at 18 to 20 years of age.

I was put to one side with the few quiet cattle that the cut out animals would be pushed to join. So I had a good view of the face, or area in front of the camp, and I could watch Jim and the other bloke cut out.

They made it look easy. They would pick out a cow and calf and move them to the front of the mob, and then the horse would back up and push the calf towards the cow when it stopped. If the cow moved, the horse would accelerate to slow the cow down so that the calf could catch up. The idea was to keep them together so that when they were clear of the mob, one of the stockmen could move in and take the cow and calf over to where they could see the other mob. Then they would trot quietly over to them.

It sounds easy but the horse was spinning and turning in every direction. Jim was doing a good job but all eyes were on the bloke without a bridle and his hands on the pommel of the saddle, working the mare with only his legs. The way the horse was moving, it was magic. I got ticked off for not keeping the mob under control and told to stop watching and get to work.

Late in the afternoon Jim called out to me to come and take a cow and calf from him.

I kicked my horse out and came up behind Jim, and as the cow took off so did the horse. I was thrown to the back of the saddle and as I clawed my way back into it we were right up to the cow and calf. I flew out to the end of the split reins but the horse just managed to catch me. Then the calf stopped, the horse stopped in mid-stride and I was sitting on his head. We had the cow and calf away from the face and I thought that everything was all right and I could relax.

But the calf ducked back and so did the horse, leaving me suspended in mid-air, holding reins which went back between my legs. I crashed into the bulldust in a heap but it didn't end there because the horse was still after the calf and I was still holding the reins in my hand. I was dragged along the ground and my mouth, my clothes and glasses became coated in dust and shit.

'Great piece of riding, Doc! I bet you can't do that again,' Jim said as he rode up to make sure that the horse was all right. And I thought that even though I had been riding horses in the bush in New South Wales since my childhood, none of them could ever have matched these agile, intelligent Gulf Country horses.

Drovers' Games

The drovers were another group of people that the station managers and head stockman always used to worry about.

Drovers were a group of blokes who kept to themselves most of the time as they were always on the move. It was only during the wet season that they went home for any length of time. We all looked forward to the news they had gathered on their travels. Some of the drovers carried messages from friends and mates who were in southern Queensland and the Northern Territory. Most of them were top bushmen and, of course, good riders.

From Dalgonally Australian Estates would send store cattle to be fattened in southern Queensland at a property called Mt Howard. This was a drive of eight to 12 weeks.

The main drovers were Tiddley Triffard and his older brother, Ted. Each had a droving plant. They didn't see each other much as they were always travelling with stock, so they would leave messages and horses for each other at different stations. This practice was frowned on by the company as the drovers' horses seemed to get serviced by the station stallion and the station always seemed to be looking after a large mob of horses they didn't own. The drovers would cut and brand their foals using the station yards, then leave them running with the station mob until they were old enough to break in.

This meant a smart drover was breeding hundreds of horses without owning a property.

Whenever a mob was being taken across the property the manager would send two or three ringers to give them a hand, mainly to stop the drovers killing the station stock for meat and to make sure they didn't take any of our stock with them. The drover was paid by the number of head he delivered and he was given a number of head to use as 'killers' on the road. So if he killed and ate someone else's cattle he would arrive with more cattle.

Drovers had many skills and the stations used to pay for these skills while the drovers were waiting for the mob to be made up.

Ted Triffard arrived with his plant not long after I arrived on Dalgonally. He was quite a serious middle-aged man and this time he arrived early to repair and recanterline the station's saddles. I was sent to give him a hand.

Leather work is very satisfying and I found a good teacher in Ted. He was strict and didn't allow any slacking. I learnt to cut and dress leather and greenhide to make ropes and halters, sew new bridles and repair old saddles. It was a good time, sitting in the shade of the shed looking out at the horse yards and the horse paddock beyond with Ted telling me in a quiet voice about some of his adventures as a drover — stories of floods, fire, drought, rushing cattle and bucking horses. He told these stories all day. They were sprinkled with short lectures to me, so I would learn to be a good stockman.

His ringers went out with the station ringers to help muster the cattle they would be droving down through Queensland to Mt Howard. The counting of large mobs of cattle was carried out with the counters (at least two) sitting on their horses while the other ringers moved the mob past them making sure they thinned out so not many went by at a time. The counters would tie a knot in the end of their whips every time they got to 50. If there were more than were wanted after counting we would cut out the ones that weren't required. You could tell that a lot of the horses Ted had in his plant were sired by the stallion on Dalgonally, they were very Arab and looked like their sire.

We got the mob together and Ted took charge and headed out. The day after he left his brother turned up. Tiddley was as different from Ted as chalk from cheese. He was a wild man who was always making bets and dares with all the station ringers, and his mares seemed to always get into the stallions' paddock. He was dark-haired and wiry, all muscle and no fat. His shirt was always hanging out and it always looked as if his clothes were falling off. His movements were swift and sure. Around horses he was a wizard, he seemed to be able to get them to do anything that he wanted. He showed me that you must teach a horse, not break it, to do the things you wanted.

One morning I was over helping to draft the brood mares, their foals and the yearlings through the yard. We had separated the yearlings, around 30 of them, into a yard on their own. They were frightened so they were milling around, pushing and shoving all around the small yard.

'Okay, who will bet I can't crawl in that yard and bite the rear hocks of those horses and not get kicked? Come on, who's going to bet me?' Tiddley was standing on the rails of the yard yelling to all of us. 'All right, I bet none of you can!'

As none of us wanted to get our heads kicked off, we all started to bet that he couldn't. By the time we were finished there was a large sum riding on the outcome.

Tiddley jumped down off the rails, took his belt with his knives and watch off, then lay down on the ground and slowly crawled through the bottom rails into the yard of horses. The dust was rising, so Tiddley was only a shadow on the ground. I thought some of the horses trod on him. They were still moving around kicking up the dust.

Neeeeehhhhh! One of the yearlings let out a yell of surprise and her back legs flashed up into the sunlight as she kicked out with both barrels. We couldn't see much through the dust, so we climbed down and watched through the lower rails.

I could see Tiddley lying down. He had his mouth open and was about to bite this horse's hock. The action was fast — he bit, then dropped his head to the ground, the horse jumped forward and kicked out. When a horse kicks out their hooves go upwards, so the hooves missed Tiddley's head by a cigarette paper. Tiddley did it a number of times until Jim turned up and yelled out for him not to upset the other horses — Jim felt it was teaching them to kick anything that was behind them.

Strange Bedfellow

I was new to the ways of the cattle camp and I had a lot to learn. One lesson was taught in a way I would never forget.

I found it very difficult to get up early in the morning when I first went out to the camp. We camped on the ground, which I found very hard after the soft bed of my childhood home in Sydney. Working all day in the saddle was something I wasn't used to either, so I would wake up in the morning with my body aching all over, and because I was so buggered at night I would hit the swag fast asleep. In the morning we would be wakened by the blare of the cook's radio and lie in our swags listening to the milking hour program. All the songs seemed to be dedicated to some very strange people who had written in requesting things like 'The Drover's Lament' and other sad country and western songs. This recital started at around four in the morning, while the cook crashed and grunted his way around as he prepared breakfast.

The next thing to wake us, if we had been fortunate enough to go back to sleep, was the horse tailer. The noise he made collecting his gear and clomping off to get the night horse made it clear that it was nearly time to get up. At our first call at five o'clock, it was still cold and dark. Sometimes I would pretend to be asleep. This would give me another few minutes in my swag, but if I didn't get up quickly the whole world would fall on me

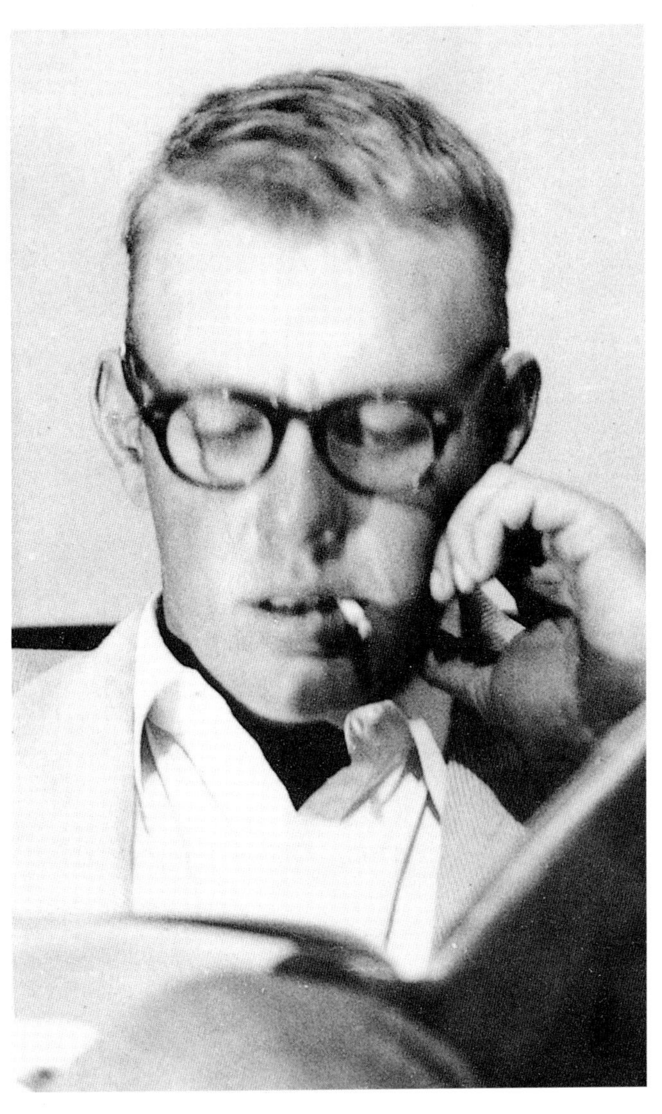

Me at the tender age of 16 and a half on Granada.

Short horn cattle was the type of cattle we bred and raised. This photo shows some of the breeding stock on Granada.

Members of the mustering camp at Granada.

Slim, lean me at 17 with my favourite mare, Diddle Dum.

My first made-to-measure Winniky Saddle on an ex-brumby stallion.

The cook's daughter in my chaps!!!!

Horsebreaker Al Milne with a young foal's first handling.

The cook's daughter flirting with us on the shed roof.

In the bed of the Leichhardt River during the dry season.

A waterhole in the gidgee scrub. We used to muster cattle into these because they would walk toward water, making it easy for us.

Bogged on my own.

The ringers' and jackaroos' kitchen and dining room on Granada.

Johnny Long killing and dressing a pig for the station.

Pushing cattle up into the crush to check them.

Cutting three-year-old bulls in the crush on Granada, an unusual sight even then.

in the form of one of the ringers who would pull the blankets off and throw a pannikin of water over me, so I had to judge my sleep-ins with precision.

Every morning, as a green stockman, I would be told 'Roll up your swag and strap it up or something might get in there. And it looks bloody untidy.'

I thought they were only nagging me about being untidy, so I didn't bother to roll my swag.

A week after one of these tirades, we had been working in the yards all day and I was stuffed — I could hardly eat my tea without falling asleep. While the others sat around talking I headed for my swag. I managed to get my boots off, then I slid into the blankets with my clothes still on, dirty as they were. I got my feet down to the bottom of the swag and there seemed to be a lump but I thought it was only some of my clothes I had left there. I was nearly asleep when I felt something slide up my body between my clothes and the blanket. I broke into a cold sweat.

What the bloody hell was it?

I lay still, not game to call out. I had worked out what it was in a flash. It stopped moving. I was on my back so whatever it was now lay along my body and up on to my chest — and I could still feel more of it at my feet. I stopped breathing.

I lay for a long time wondering what to do, then because I had to breathe I decided to have a look. I slowly moved the blanket down my chest. In the moonlight I could see pretty well and I was more than wide awake by this time, but I was completely unprepared for what happened next.

I came face to face with the head of the largest snake I had ever seen! It was lying on my chest and looking me in the eye, with its black forked tongue flickering in and out of its mouth, nearly touching my face.

'Yyyyyyeeeeeeee!'

With a yell that was more like a scream I jumped out of those blankets without touching them. I don't think the snake felt me leave, I moved so fast.

I stood there shaking about 20 feet away from my swag and through my shock I heard the sound of laughter. I turned towards the fire and there were all the ringers, laughing their guts out. I backed further away from my swag as I couldn't see the snake, at the same time yelling that I could have been bitten and telling them in unprintable terms what I thought of them.

One of the ringers came over and pulled the blanket back and there, lying half uncoiled, was a ten foot plains python who didn't look at all worried as the ringer carried him out into some scrub land and let him go.

'Now will you learn to pick your clothes up off the ground and roll and strap your swag? Next time it won't be us with a harmless python.' It was Jim who said that. He was right again, of course, which was proved a couple of months later when one of the ringers got stung by a scorpion that had got into his swag. He had to be rushed back to the station and flown to Cloncurry.

Rats, Big as Bloody Cats, Everywhere

The milking session on the radio and the news at night warned us that a rat plague was on its way towards us, so we made sure that all the food, meat and leather gear was stored so that the rats couldn't eat it. We sat around the fire worrying about the news and wondering when the rats would come.

One morning there were no rats and late that night there were rats everywhere. I was awakened by a sharp bite on my nose. Half asleep, I hit out and my hand came in contact with a furry object. I opened my eyes to look at a rat's face about to sink his teeth into my hand. I grabbed one of my riding boots that were always close by and hit the rat before it bit me. Bloody hell!

I looked around and could see things moving all around my swag — no, not just around my swag. The whole camp site seemed to be alive.

I jumped up, stood on my swag to put my boots on and kicked my way through the furry tide to the fire where I found all the camp sitting around drinking tea because the rats had woken them up and driven them from their swags as well. It was a long night because we couldn't get back into our swags — the rats had taken them over.

After that first night we set up our mossie nets and tucked them in all round our swags and that seemed to stop them —

most of them. They got into everything that was lying around. Whenever we picked up a sack or a camp oven, the rats would jump out from underneath in their dozens.

After dinner at night we made up a game. We would sit in a large circle in the dark and place some food scraps in the middle. We would all be armed with a metre-long piece of number eight wire. We would hold this up above our heads and as the rats moved in to eat the scraps we would bring the wire down fast, sometimes killing up to three at a time. We would take turns and the one with the biggest pile of dead rats in the end won.

Some nights we would kill 300 between us. The next morning, if we had a late start or a day off, we would spend hours tossing the dead rats' carcasses into the air for the diving kite hawks who would blacken the sky over the camp. Some of these birds would dive down from great heights to pluck a rat out of the air. It was great fun to watch the aerial display these birds put on.

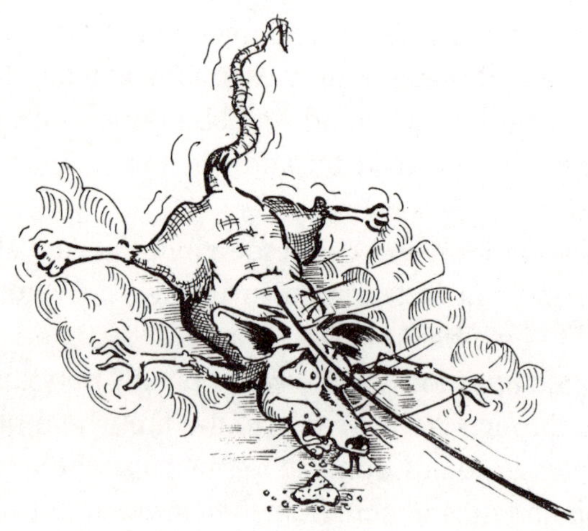

I'm Dreaming of a White Christmas

We had taken the mustering camp out to the north-western corner of the property, about 30 miles from the homestead and there were just black soil plains between us and it. We had set up camp at an old boundary rider's hut. It was a small one-roomed affair with a verandah out the front, so we erected a tent fly out from the back wall for the kitchen. The head stockman and the cook slept inside the hut, so the cook could start cooking before dawn without waking us. The rest of us slept in our swags under the stars. The whole area around us was hill and ridge country covered with gidgee scrub, ant hills and spinifex.

We were supposed to be there for two weeks mustering, yarding up and branding, then bringing the fat cattle in to the station so the buyers could come out and look them over. The first week went well and we were running ahead of time.

The clouds started to build up but we didn't worry as the wet season was three months away. We could expect a shower or two, which would make the mustering harder, since the cattle wouldn't be walking towards the waterholes. They would be content to find water out where they were grazing, so we would have a hard time moving them. Some of the ringers wanted to stop and head into the station, but Jim, the head stockman, said we only had a few days in which to muster and if we left then we would have to muster the whole area again if the wet came early.

The sheet lightning, thunder and black clouds had us worried about getting back to the homestead. We got into it with a vengeance but on the last two days of yard work the rain came pouring down. We got the drafting finished and headed back to the camp, hoping the rain would stop so that we that could complete the branding. But the next day the rain was even heavier. Jim made the decision to let the cattle out so we could make a run for the station.

While some of us went to let the cattle out, two of the ringers went down the road towards the station to see what the black plains were like for the four-wheel drive vehicle and the horses. We had just moved the last of the cattle from the yards when they came galloping back.

'The whole area in the direction of the station is under water,' one of the ringers told Jim. We all wanted to see, so we rode down through the gidgee to the open country. An amazing sight met our eyes. There were waves breaking along the shore of a huge expanse of water stretching as far as the eye could see and the dry, cracked black soil plain had turned into an inland sea. It was over 20 miles to the station through the Channel Country and it was still raining.

Jim sent some riders in the direction of Cloncurry but they were back before dark and said that all the creeks were running bankers and the river was too wide and fast to swim the horses. They had swum a few creeks to get that far and they were cold, wet and hungry. At first we sat around during the day enjoying the break, repairing our clothes and gear and plaiting leather. Some of the others played cards but then the tobacco ran out and tempers started to fray. The ringers were trying to smoke anything from dried cow dung to bark.

There were ten ringers and five Aborigines all trying to

shelter in the hut and on the verandah. It had been raining heavily (a record 21 inches of rain fell altogether) for a week when the cook informed us that all our fresh food, sugar, flour and tea was finished. Fights were breaking out and I got into trouble because I was a know-all and wouldn't stop talking. Those ringers could go for days without saying a word but I had to fill any silence with chatter, most of it about myself and my knowledge since I wanted everyone to take notice of me. (This has brought me undone quite a few times.)

'Shut up, Doc. If you say another word about how you can swim I'll flatten you,' Jim yelled across the small space of the hut.

'I can outswim you,' I answered back before I could stop myself.

'Okay, that's it, come here.' He leapt up and grabbed me by the arm as I tried to get away. 'See that flooded creek — you swim over and back for a week's wages.'

I looked in horror at the creek. It was running a banker and there were branches and rubbish roaring down in the turbulence. I realised that Jim meant me to say no, lose a week's pay and shut up.

'Okay, you're on!' (I think the wet had affected my brain.) The ringers were all excited and making bets, some betting that I wouldn't try it, others that I wouldn't make it. My few friends were betting that I could do it.

Jim wanted me to put a rope around my waist but I wouldn't hear of it. It must have made a funny sight, the cook and the ringers slipping and sliding through the rain down the hill to the edge of the water to watch me take up the challenge.

'Doc, you don't have to,' said Jim as he unrolled his rope, ready to throw to me in case I got into trouble.

'No, I'll be right,' I said with more confidence than I felt. Now I could see the speed of the water and the size of the objects that were coming down with it. I walked along the bank and up the creek until I came to the fence which used to run across it. Then I started to wade out. The water was light brown and I had to feel the bottom as I couldn't see my feet. Where the current was strongest I looked upriver to make sure that no debris was coming before starting out. It looked all clear, so I dived in.

The current grabbed me immediately and started to sweep me downstream. I started to swim with all my might. The current was a lot stronger than I had imagined and I was swept past where the ringers were all standing (no, not standing, they were jumping up and down and waving). I thought that they were encouraging me but as I touched the bottom on the other side, I was lifted off my feet and pushed down into the mud on the bottom by a great weight. I started to panic — I was being held down face first on the muddy bottom.

Then the weight started to shift, going slowly over my back. I struggled to the surface and took in large lungfuls of air. Then my feet were on the bottom and I was out of the current on the other side. I looked down the creek in time to see a huge tree trunk disappearing around the bend. I sat down and started to shiver as the reaction to my near miss set in.

Jim was yelling and shouting but I couldn't hear him through the noise of the rushing water. He was waving and gesturing for me to swim back. I got up and walked back up the creek bank, then waded in. I knew I didn't want to swim across — that tree trunk had frightened me a lot. But the whole camp was on the other bank, waving and jumping up and down and taking bets, so I thought, 'here goes nothing' and dived out as far as I could. I was doing all right until I was halfway, then my leg started to cramp. The pain was terrible. I tried to keep going but I knew I was going to be lucky if I made it.

Splash! I was swimming in a tangle of rope. I managed to grab hold of it and was quickly pulled to the bank, where about three of the stockmen caught hold of me and carried me out.

'Well, you don't have to worry about the horse this time,' I said to Jim sarcastically, which he didn't really appreciate!

Everyone else, apart from me, was talking and having a good time in the rain on the slippery creek bank. I was just tired and wet.

The rain finally stopped and after a week of dry weather and a diet of old cow — the cow had staggered past and had been filled with lead by a mad visiting Yank stockman with an automatic rifle — the head stockman, myself and two other ringers caught some horses and tried to cross the black soil plains to get help.

The plains still looked like an inland sea, with water to the horizon. The water wasn't deep but the mud was, up to the horses' bellies, and they got knocked up only about a mile out from the shore. We were lucky to get them back in. They were buggered by the time they got back to dry land. Some of us had to use our spurs to make them move out of the mud and, after that, we rode back disheartened and muddy into camp. Jim was hoping the station manager would help us out, since the situation was starting to get quite serious as the days went on. We only had the old cow to eat and not much else.

But one morning we were awakened by the noise of a low-flying Cessna plane buzzing the camp. We jumped up and headed for the cattle yards where we had laid out the word 'FOOD' written with bags and clothes in the large main yard. The plane flew over a number of times, then roared down over us, dipped its wings and headed away into the distance.

The next day we listened for the sound of that engine but it wasn't until the second day that the plane returned. We were all excited as we raced down to the yards, climbed up and sat waiting on the top rails as the plane came in low over our heads. We all held our breath. Two large bags came tumbling down out of the door and, spot on, they hit our sign.

Poooooffffffft! We were shrouded in a cloud of white flour. When it settled, we were all white from head to foot and looked like strange snowmen. The Aborigines looked like black and white minstrels. The plane dipped its wings and an upraised finger was seen at the pilot's window — !!!!!!!!!

The rest of the drop went without a hitch. One box was dropped attached to a homemade parachute and to our surprise on opening it, we found a cheering note from the station women and a large fruit cake. We stood, covered in flour, and scoffed the lot. They had thought to put tobacco, papers and matches in one of the bags, so tempers cooled.

It took over two weeks for the plain to be passable. Even then the horses were stuffed from their ordeal and as they topped the station ridge they were happy to see home. We stockmen were met by a manager who wasn't too sympathetic. It was a tired mob of ringers who unsaddled and climbed into the truck for the short run to the station — and an even more tired and sore cook. He didn't usually ride and had to be helped off his horse and into the truck. For the next week he lay around, whingeing a lot about his aches and pains.

A Crafty Bastard

The role of night horses in the stock camp is to muster the riding horses out of the large horse paddock in the early morning. The night horses were kept in a small paddock about half a mile square with their front legs hobbled and a bell around their neck so you could catch them easily. These horses were old, quiet and cunning. I am sure they spent their waking hours dreaming up games and tricks they could play on unsuspecting, sleepy jackaroos before dawn.

When my turn to catch the night horse came around the camp cook would shake me awake. Sitting up in my swag, I would pull on my R M Williams riding boots, roll and secure my swag, collect the night horse's bridle and then walk out into the darkness and start looking for the bastard in the darkest, largest paddock in the world — that's what it seemed like to me.

The first thing you would do is make your way to the middle of the paddock, stand very still and listen for the bell or jingle of the hobbles. If that didn't work you would search the paddock and as dawn broke you would crouch down and look around to see if you could spot the horse outlined against the skyline.

These horses were much too cunning for that. I remember one, an old brown gelding named Toby, who drove me and the head stockman mad my first month at the mustering camp.

The first time I went to catch him it took about an hour. He had filled his bell and covered his hobbles with mud, and as I walked one way, swearing, he would quietly hop the other way, keeping his front feet together to make no noise and moving very slowly so he circled around me.

It was only with dawn and the head stockman bellowing for me to stop stuffing around out there and catch the f ...king thing and get the horses in since the whole camp had had breakfast and was waiting to go mustering, that I saw the cunning old bastard sneak behind a prickly bush. I soon caught him and walked him back to where my saddle was hanging on the fence near the gate.

As I was saddling up the head stockman came across and said, 'Next time, as soon as you catch him, don't lead him up to your saddle, hop on him bareback and ride him. It won't take as long.'

The next time he was hiding behind a tree way down at the far end of the night paddock. I caught him, took the hobbles off and tied them around his neck, then slipped on him bareback and kicked him in the ribs.

That was it. He leapt into the air — fffaaaaaaarrrrrrtttttt — with a huge fart and started to pigroot all around the place. I was on his neck one minute, his bum the next, all the time yelling at the top of my voice for him to stop and telling him in rough terms what would happen to him if he didn't. With that he threw me into a prickly bush, whinnied, threw his head into the air and galloped off. Without the hobbles it took the whole camp an hour to catch him — and I got a lecture from the head stockman for upsetting a quiet night horse.

Rawhide

Night horses were more important when droving. They were picked for their night vision and were only used when you rode around the cattle at night to stop them wandering away. You would sing to the cattle all the time so they would not spook and rush, because every night these cattle were on strange night camps any sudden noise or movement could set them going. The first night was the worst and the drover would ask the head stockman if he could use six or eight men from the camp for the first few nights, or until the cattle were off their own pasture.

At first I used to badger the head stockman to let me go out on the road. After nine months he relented and said I could go with the drover Tiddley Triffard to Gilliat, the closest rail to Dalgonally. We would take our time on the trip, moving the mob slowly so they wouldn't lose any condition. This was the first time I went droving off the station with another group of blokes. After all the tales I had heard of Tiddley and his drovers this was it — high adventure!

I rolled my swag and threw it in the back of the drovers' truck, then headed out to the mob on one of their horses. We were taking a 1000 head mob to Gilliat so they could be trucked into Townsville. We would only be on the road for about a week.

The head stockman and the rest of the camp stayed with us the first night. I sat around the fire listening to the stories of horse-breaking, borrowing horses, cattle duffers and, of course, cattle rushes. I was told always to sleep with my feet at the bottom of a tree, because if the cattle rushed it wasn't like in the movies where they would get up slowly, then canter away.

In real life there was a crack like a huge whip, then the sound of thunder as they rushed off into the distance. If you were unlucky then they would rush straight over the camp but that wasn't often, they assured me. To be safe you slept with your feet at the base of a tree so you might just make it up the tree out of the way of the rush. If there were no trees then you should sleep near a night horse which was saddled and ready to go.

The other thing to remember if you were moving around the mob in the dark was to talk to yourself or sing so the cattle knew where you were all the time and wouldn't get a fright. My songs were different to the others' country and western songs. I sang rock 'n' roll but after a while I changed to songs like 'I'll Walk the Line', 'Sixteen Tons', 'Don't Ever Take the Ribbon From Your Hair', 'Rawhide' and 'Water, Clear, Cool Water'. I still remember most of the words because there were always song books around the camp.

The first night I was keyed up, expecting anything to happen. Because we had the drover's men and the mustering camp ringers we only had short watches. I found the night horses amazing — they could actually see in the dark. When you were walking around the cattle, every now and then the night horse would head out into the dark away from the mob. At first I tried to turn the horse back but it would keep going and suddenly you would come across a beast trying to walk away in the dark. The horse would keep a good distance so as not to frighten the animal, I wouldn't stop singing and together we would turn the animal back into the mob without disturbing the rest.

The next morning the station ringers had breakfast with us and helped with the mob to the boundary, then said their farewells and headed back towards the mustering camp. The drovers' truck and the horse tailer had gone ahead to find a good night camp.

I soon found that droving cattle was not like mustering where you mustered the cattle together and pushed them as fast as possible in a day so you could yard them. Droving is more like just following the cattle as they graze and all you have to do is keep the stragglers up with the main mob and keep them all pointed in the right direction. We would only be travelling 12 to 14 miles a day.

Drovers can sleep in the saddle because the horses feed and move backwards and forwards across the back of the mob without guidance. I found myself drifting in and out of daydreams as we made our way slowly through the scrub.

Lunch was in our saddle bags: damper and meat and strong black tea with plenty of sugar. Sitting around, eating lunch, I learnt more about watching the cattle at night.

'If the cattle ever rush, lie along your horse's neck and don't try to guide him because he can see. He'll keep out on the wing of the cattle until they start to slow down, then he'll move in on the leaders and turn them in on themselves until they stop. Don't try to move them, just hold them until we're all there,' Tiddley said. 'Then we hold them until morning, count them and then muster the rest. They normally stay together, so it's not too bad. While we're doing this the mob is just eating and relaxing, so we shouldn't have any more trouble.'

I thought that sounded a little too easy — and how right I was.

We were two nights out. It was around two o'clock in the morning, the cattle had been restless as there were a lot of dingoes howling and moving around, and some of the cattle were trying to walk back towards home. I was on watch and trying to turn back these cattle on the opposite side of the mob to the camp, so I don't know what spooked them.

Craaaaaackkkkkk!

It sounded as if a huge whip had gone off, or like thunder when you are right under the lightning. The cattle were lying down one minute, then en masse they hit their feet and were off like a brown wave through the trees away from me. My heart was in my mouth. I could feel the night horse gathering up under me and then it took off after the mob. I can tell you I was scared. I couldn't see where we were going but I could hear the cattle crashing and calling in front of me.

The only thing I could do was lie along the horse's back, give it its head and hope for the best. The horse was racing through the darkness and I could hear the cattle on my left, which meant I was on the creek side of the mob. I was all over the horse's back, one minute up on his neck, the next on his rump. Every few moments the horse would gather himself and then leap into the air. I don't know how, but I stayed with him. I think I knew if I fell off I would be hurt and I knew that we were jumping erosions, God knows how deep. I just hoped and prayed the horse wouldn't lose his footing.

Once I thought we had bought it — his front legs went out from underneath him. I sat back and gathered him back up on his feet and only got my head down when a branch cracked me with such force that I was nearly knocked from the saddle. My ears were ringing but through the din I could hear someone yelling up ahead. Suddenly we were next to a rider.

'Yell your head off. We're right up with the leaders and if we turn them over to the left out of this broken country we should be able to hold them together.'

I lost sight of him as the darkness and dust closed in around me. The night horse knew what to do so I started to yell at the cattle to turn them away from the gullies and erosions. The horse and I broke free from the scrub and my eyes seemed to have gained night vision so I could see that we were galloping right alongside the leaders. Without the trees I could use my stockwhip, so I started to crack it for all I was worth. I thought I was starting to turn the cattle when the rest of the drovers appeared out of the darkness and with all of us there it wasn't long before we had wheeled them back and they were just milling around.

'We'll hold them here until sun-up, so it's no sleep for any of us,' Tiddley said as he rode past. 'You did well, Doc, now you know what a rush is all about.'

We held the cattle for the rest of the night and in the morning strung them out along the track so that they could be counted. We had lost around 50 head, so two of us were sent back with our rifles to shoot any injured cattle and to look for the missing ones.

Riding back, we came across some badly injured cattle. Most had fallen into the gullies. We found the tracks of my horse out wide and I must admit that I went grey when I saw the jumps we had taken in our mad ride. Later, as an experienced rider, I would not have attempted to ride flat gallop over a course like that and I suddenly had a lot more respect for the good old night horse.

By the time we had mustered the stragglers we found we had only lost around six head but some of the ones we moved back to the herd were a bit lame and some had big wounds along their sides. We were very lucky that no-one had been hurt. We didn't move far that day because the cattle were tired. So we just let them graze while we took turns to lie in the shade of a tree and catch up on some sleep, only getting up to turn some of the cattle back if they strayed too far out.

We had to hold the cattle in the Gilliat common as the train was a week late, which wasn't unusual up there.

Balls and All

After yarding up a large mob of cattle the job of branding, earmarking and cutting started. It was hot, dry and very dusty running around in the yards pushing cattle from one yard to the yard where they were to be drafted. I found my legs ached from running in high-heeled riding boots — they are not the things to wear while working on the ground.

We would draft all the calves into one yard and then when we had them separated from their mothers we would force them into a crush which led to a calf cradle. This is a two-sided affair which we would slam closed on the calf, then with two of us pulling together we would pull calf and cradle to the ground. The calf was now held securely on its side so we could work on it. Close by would be the branding fire with the station brands and year number sitting white-hot, waiting for the brander to grab them and hit the calf with them, leaving a permanent brand on the calf's hide. The smell of burning hair and hide was thick in the air. Added to this the flies, heat, dust and the screams of the calves made it work that we hurried to get finished.

Before branding we would castrate the bull calves, followed by earmarking. This meant, to make the calf's life more miserable, you would take a large chunk out of its ear with the earmarking pliers. The calf would bellow and kick as this was being done. It took less than a minute to perform these tasks. We would spring open the cradle and let the calf up, and the cradle was then in place for the next calf.

We would be racing around with hot brands and pliers yelling at each other to move it and get out of the way. There were some near misses with the branding iron. Sometimes a large bull calf would get through the cradle. He would charge through and we wouldn't have the strength to stop him. We would have to rope and throw him. It helped to break the routine up.

The first time I worked on a large mob I noticed the ringer who was cutting out the balls hand them to the Aborigines who were working on the crush and keeping the fire going.

'Hey, what are they going to do with the balls?' I asked one of the ringers.

'You'll see.'

I noticed they were placing the newly removed calf balls on hot stones beside the branding fire. They looked like sausages.

Sausages!!!!!!!!! Oh no, they weren't going to eat them!

A black ringer moved one of the balls out of the heat by pushing his knife into it. He blew on it to cool it, then took a bite. I watched in horror as he munched away.

'Come on, Doc, try some,' the ringer said, smiling as he held one out to me on the end of his knife.

'What do they taste like?' I asked, hoping the head stockman would send me to the other end of the yards so that I wouldn't have to try them. That didn't happen so I took the cooling ball off the knife and held it in my hand. Looking round, I could see that everyone was watching to see what I would do.

What could I do? I was standing with a ball in my hand and the calf whose ball I had was watching me from the other side of the yard, looking a little hurt.

Well, here goes nothing. I took a bite. Its texture was a little crunchy and to my surprise it tasted like sausage. The ringers were a little disappointed that I liked it.

After that there was always a fight to see who got the biggest ones. When the balls were nearly cooked the Aborigines would jump down off the crush rails where they were working and make a dash over to the fire to try to grab the biggest ones before we could. We would get into fun fights trying to stop each other from getting the best ones and the head stockman would get mad because we weren't getting the job done.

If a young bull had been giving us trouble before being cut, the ringer who was eating his balls would taunt the now cut and docile steer by running up to it and making a great show of how good his balls were to eat.

After we had our fill we would throw the balls up in the air for the ever-present kite hawks.

From Here to Eternity

The most wonderful time in the mustering camp for me — and I never got sick of it — was when I went to my swag, away from the light of the camp fire, to where I couldn't hear the other ringers talking. I would lie down and relax, looking up into the night sky.

Most of the year the night sky in the Gulf would be cloudless. It was like a huge piece of dark blue velvet which had been stretched from one horizon to the other and sprinkled with gold dust, mostly thin and sparkly but in some areas so thick that it looked like solid gold. Because the country was so flat I could see the earth curving away all around me. The night sky took up everything I could see.

I would look up and think about the things I had been taught: 'If you look up into the night sky you are only seeing one galaxy. Beyond this one are hundreds and thousands of them and they stretch to eternity.'

Eternity. What's that? My mind could not comprehend the thought of eternity as I lay there looking up at millions of stars. I had always believed that everything had a beginning and an end. Trees, animals and humans all had a birth and a death. But here, all around me, was something that had been here always and went on forever.

As my gaze took in the sky, I imagined the same number of

stars and planets that I could see occurring again, then again and yet again. As I travelled further and further out in my mind I found myself getting smaller and smaller. I would stop thinking about it only when I felt I was the size of a grain of dust. I would get worried about how infinitesimal our world and we really are in the system of things. Sometimes the thoughts made my head spin and I would put my head under the blankets to block it all out. At other times I marvelled at the size of the universe and wondered if it was only atoms in a giant's drink and all the length of our existence was only the time He took to pour and drink it.

On the Road Again

I was called to the manager's office after breakfast one morning and informed that I was going to be transferred to a station called Granada. I was disappointed and asked why. The manager told me that head office had requested the move. They thought that a change of scenery would do me the world of good and get me away from one of the house girls that I was seeing. The station I was being sent to had no black workers.

I was to pack immediately because I would be leaving that day with him. He was driving over to Canobie Station for a managers' conference and the manager of Granada would be there to take me on to Granada.

I raced around the station saying goodbye to everyone I could, as some of them were away at the mustering camps. Everyone gave me a present — the one I remember was the set of leather bound classics Ted, the old windmill expert, gave me. I read them over and over again during the next few years.

Well, I was off on another adventure to Granada. I had heard a bit about it — it was a herd bull stud 200 square miles in area. The homestead was on the Dugard River and most of the country was flat, with black soil plains and gidgee scrub. I heard the manager was one for everyone staying on their proper level.

I was a bit sad as I watched the homestead disappear into the shimmering heat, I had learnt a lot in the year I had been there.

There were three of us in the ute — me on the back, and the manager and Jim Mitchell in the front. I had to hop out to open and close the gates, so by the time I got to Canobie I was covered in dust and sweat, not a pretty sight.

Before I could clean up I found myself being introduced to Mr Robert Scandred, the manager of Granada Station. He was of medium height and thickset. He was wearing a tweed sports coat, woollen tie and flat broad-brimmed hat, and he was smoking a pipe. I could feel his disapproval of my ringer's outfit. I wasn't dressed as a jackaroo should be when travelling around and meeting the heads of stations. Jim gave him a rundown on what I could do and how I had learnt a lot about moving cattle.

So on the way home Mr Scandred gave me the first of many lectures about my dress and how I was a representative of the company and should act accordingly.

The camp at Granada was quite small, with just the Long brothers, John Bennett, Barry the head stockman, Allen Milne, Bert the cook and me.

It was at this time that I bought some horses, two stock ponies that had just been broken in. One was named Diddle Dum and the other Peggy. Diddle Dum's name came from the way she galloped — diddly dum, diddly dum, diddly dum. She was around 15 hands and bay coloured. She was good-natured and I used to spend a lot of time with her.

Peggy's name came from the rock 'n' roll song 'Peggy Sue, I Love You'. She was good-natured but full of beans. In the morning when I first climbed aboard she used to like to rock 'n' roll. She was a little fatter than Diddle Dum — but I never told her that!

Out at the camp we had an old boundary rider's hut with a verandah back and front. It was set in the night paddock with the horse yards and an earth turkey nest behind. In front there was a fence and then the horse paddock. If we were home early we would get the newly broken horses which Allen Milne, the horse breaker, had delivered out to us, saddle them up and ride them. Sometimes after a day's work we would take them out, with one of us riding an old horse, and teach them to go in the direction that we wanted. It looked comical, horses cantering around with their heads turned into their shoulders and still going straight ahead. You had to be very calm, as some of the young horses had strong wills.

It was in this camp that we all ganged up against the head stockman, Barry, for cruelty to horses and cattle. He was the first and only person in the Gulf who I saw being cruel to animals.

Because we had to muster all the horses to get the young ones, when we got back and let the young horses go, a lot of the other horses would be grazing in front of the hut. I would get some sugar or damper and call Peggy and Diddle Dum and they would always come cantering up. I would sit on them without a bridle or saddle and guide them around with my knees, using their manes. This was great fun. The rest of the camp would be sitting on the verandah drinking tea and telling me how to make them back up and do a few tricks.

One afternoon I was doing this and without warning, Barry crept up and whipped his red hide reins down on Diddle Dum's rump with all his might.

With a whinny Diddle Dum shot away. I was sitting on her back and only had time to grab a couple of handfuls of mane and jam my legs hard into her ribs, which only made her go faster. I pulled myself up and laid my head down near her head and tried to soothe her. We were flying, the wind was streaming past my face and we were in open country so I thought I would let her run herself out. There really wasn't anything else that I could do, I had already tried pulling on her mane and yelling but it hadn't made the slightest difference.

Looking ahead, I saw that Diddle Dum had seen a mob of horses feeding, and between them and us was a large erosion. I got worried and started to talk faster and pull on her mane. She thought it was a challenge so she picked up speed. We were committed. The erosion looked wider and deeper than I would ever try to jump — and that's with a saddle and bridle, not riding bareback with a handful of mane. Christ! It was deep, we were going to get very hurt if we didn't make the jump.

But then, suddenly, we were over, I was still on board and we were streaking towards the other horses — a wall of horses was in front of us. I think I closed my eyes for a second. Then we were through them and heading towards the camp. Diddle Dum didn't let up and I knew she was mad at me as we thundered over the plain towards the night paddock gate.

Oh no, the bloody gate was closed. I could see two of the ringers had seen me coming and were running to open the bloody thing. I was talking to Diddle Dum fast and gently, asking her to stop please, PLEASE! The gate was rushing up and I thought 'She's got no chance of stopping, we're committed to bloody jumping it.' I got ready to go into the air as the gate came at us. Just as I thought we were both committed to the jump, Diddle Dum put her front legs straight out in front of her and sat down on her bum. She stopped dead, up against the gate.

I flew over her head and must have sailed a good 30 feet before a prickle bush pulled me up. I looked back at Diddle Dum. She snorted and shook her head at me, turned and trotted off with her tail high in the air.

It took about ten minutes to get me out of the prickle bush.

Barry used the 'I'm the head stockman, if you hit me you get fired' routine.

We Get Our Own Back

A few days later Allen turned up with another mob of horses. One of them was a worry. Before Allen left he told Barry that it was a good horse and that he should ride it.

The next afternoon saw us in the horse yards catching our young horses to school. Of course Barry picked the one that Allen had told him about. As head stockman, he really had to pick the hardest one to handle because he couldn't ask any of the ringers to ride or handle something he couldn't. The horse was a gelding, nearly black and around sixteen and a half hands. It had certainly been gelded late, so it had lots of go and a wild look in its eye.

We saddled up and sat waiting for Barry. He was always worried about young horses because they were unpredictable. After he had finished mucking about and pulling the horse around, he got the saddle on and was feeling under its belly for the girth when suddenly it struck out with its front legs, catching Barry on the thigh, tearing his trousers and taking some skin off. (When you are on the ground one of the most dangerous actions of a horse is striking, not rearing. Striking is when the horse lifts and throws his legs out at you from a standing position, trying to strike you to the ground. This is not a common trait, thank God, and is normally only seen in horses that have been badly treated. The only way to make sure that such a horse can't strike is to stand as close as you can to his shoulder with a tight rein, so that if he tries it, you can move into his shoulder with the tight rein and he will follow you around.)

Barry was standing well away from this horse, looking very frightened. It had thrown the saddle and he was having to lead the horse around so he could retrieve the saddle from the ground, all the time worrying that the horse might jump forward and strike him down. He eventually saddled up and mounted, then took a couple of turns around the yard. The colt behaved himself and didn't do a thing wrong.

'Open the gate, Doc, and let's go,' Barry yelled at me. I tried to lean down off my horse but she was a young filly and unused to someone leaning out of the saddle so she pigrooted away. After calming her down I hopped off and opened the gate. Barry's colt came out of the yard and wouldn't turn so he kicked it hard. With that it clamped its teeth down on the bit and took off at a million miles an hour. In other words, it bolted. It had nearly unsaddled Barry as it took off, so while he was trying to get back into the saddle the horse had covered a lot of ground and was going into the gidgee scrub, where he would have no chance of stopping it.

My filly was excited and going around in circles. The other ringers were calming their horses and waiting for me to mount.

'We'd better go and see what's happening to him. There's no way we can do anything, because we're all riding half-broken horses,' John said.

'Doc's had it. Barry'll be gunning for him.'

We started the horses towards the gidgee scrub and as we came past the first trees we could see a body on the ground.

'Quick, Doc, you have the quietest horse, hop off and check him out.'

I rode as close as my horse would go, then slipped off and tied her up. I approached Barry, he was lying on his back with his eyes closed.

'How is he, Doc?'

'I don't know yet.' As I knelt down next to him I could see that he was breathing. 'He's breathing, but unconscious.'

'Give him a few minutes, he should come around. The rest of us had better hunt up the horse. It can't be left to run about with the saddle on.'

As they rode away Barry started to come around. We sat around and had a smoke, then walked back to the yards leading my horse. Half an hour later the others came back leading Barry's horse.

'He hadn't gone far — about a mile before the reins caught in a fallen tree and threw him. He was lying tangled up so we had to cut one of the reins.'

They rode into the yard and I came up and took the reins and led the horse into the small yard where I unsaddled it.

'Doc, you saddle up that horse with your gear and ride it now,' Barry said in a loud angry voice.

'Hey, the head stockman's supposed to ride all the horses and you haven't ridden this one,' one of the ringers yelled at Barry. An argument broke out and before we all got into trouble, I yelled out 'Hey, you blokes, I'll do it if that's what he wants.'

I unsaddled my horse and slowly saddled up Barry's horse, talking to him quietly all the time. I got him saddled without him striking me but it took a lot of patience. Then it was time to ride him. I put my foot in the stirrup and flew into the saddle. He pigrooted around the yard and then did the same in the larger yard. Someone handed me my stockwhip.

'Okay, let me out into the open,' I called to the ringer on the gate. I was pretty scared as we walked out the yard gate. This was my first bolter and I could feel him bunching up underneath me.

Whoooooshhhh! He was off. I yelled out for him to stop and pulled hard on the reins, but he wasn't going to stop. We were travelling at a gallop and I had to act right then. So I reversed the stockwhip handle and brought it down with all my strength between his ears.

It worked like a dream. His front legs went from under him and he skidded along the ground on his chest, with me holding his head up by the reins. By the time we came to a halt he was conscious again. He stood up and just shook. I patted him and talked softly to him until he had calmed down, then I turned and walked him back to the yards. He bunched up a few times but I only had to place the whip handle on his neck for him to settle down. I had been told to do that by a horse breaker as the last resort.

Much to our joy, Barry drove into the station and resigned. I bought the horse and he turned into a great cutting-out horse called Strike A Light — one strike of the whip and he saw the light!

Who's Who

It was a good camp on Granada, the only fly in the ointment was the manager. He was from a small property down south and he used to expect all of us to be clean and tidy, even when we were out in the mustering camps, and for me that was an impossibility. We were always to address him respectfully, no matter what the circumstances.

He had a habit of turning up when we were all stuffed, sweating and covered in bulldust. He would take the head stockman to one side and have a go about the condition we were in. The head stockman would try to please him by anwering 'Yes sir', 'No sir' or 'I'll see to it right away sir'. He would never say anything to us but he certainly gave the head stockman a bad time.

The other thing that drove us mad was just when everything was going well he would turn up and take over, telling us where we should be and how to do our work. This meant that all the work took twice as long. We used to dread seeing his ute arrive because it meant the day was going to be long and frustrating.

We had finished mustering the back paddocks and had yarded about 1500 head of cows, plus about 150 herd bulls which were in amongst the mob. The mob were all very hot and irritable. We had just dismounted and were tying our sweat-drenched horses in the shade of the few trees growing nearby so they were out of the dust that was billowing up into the sky from the yards.

As we walked over to the yards one of the ringers swore and said, 'Look out, the bloody manager's arrived. It'll take bloody hours to draft the bloody cattle with him interfering.'

Barry, the head stockman, hurried over to him, saying to us, 'Start to push the mob through the yards, I'll go and see if I can piss him off.'

While the manager and Barry were talking, we split into two groups. Some of us went to the larger yards that the cattle were already in, while the others started to open the inner yard gates so we could push the mob through to be drafted.

The old bulls and the scrubby cows were so hot and bothered that every time they caught a glimpse of us through the billowing bulldust they would charge. All around the yards you could hear yells and swearing. You only got a moment's notice when one of the cattle charged, so you would do everything by reflex as you had no time to think.

A yell of 'Look out, Doc!!' would have my legs moving at a hundred miles an hour, trying to get purchase and, without thinking, you found yourself halfway up the rails with the breeze of an enraged animal fanning your legs as it roared by. Sometimes some of the older ones couldn't stop and they would crash into the rails below you.

Some of the slimmer ringers would dive through the rails, which was alright if you were in the outer yards, but if you were diving through to another yard you could end up in more trouble than you were in before.

This particular mob seemed to be more upset than usual and there were cries of 'Look out for that mad bastard!!', 'Christ, that was close!' and 'If that old bastard doesn't calm down I'll run him up the chute and cut him'.

The dust was so thick that sometimes the mad bastards were

upon you before you could get to the safety of the rails. I found myself trying to sidestep huge, horny, cranky shapes as they hurtled through the dust. Believe me, they were motoring as they bore down on you. While they couldn't turn very well at top speed — one thing in our favour — they could hook us with their horns as they flew past. It was a great way to make a quid — run down by berserk animals, covered from head to foot in dust, flies and cow shit — we all loved it.

Looking over the yards we saw that the manager had gone back to his ute and the head stockman was heading for the drafting yard. We all climbed around to hear what he had to say.

'The manager's going to do the drafting himself, he'll tell you where he wants them.'

'Bloody hell, we'll be here 'til hell freezes over with him doing the drafting.'

'Shut up, here he comes.'

'Christ, look, he's walking through the cattle in the big yard, didn't anyone warn him about the old bull?'

We all looked across the yard from our perch on the top rails to see the manager ambling through the mob, calmly reading his notebook as if he were on a Sunday stroll. Behind him on the edge of the mob was the old bull. He had spotted the manager and was ripping great hunks of earth out of the ground with his front feet and throwing his head from side to side, not taking his beady, bloodshot eyes off the manager's back. The cloud of dust thrown up by the bull hid his body. All you could see were his huge shoulders and head with those long, sharp horns standing out of the dust.

We were all mesmerised, here was a man walking across a yard of wild, upset cattle as if he was walking down a city street with not a care in the world. The bull couldn't believe it either, he suddenly took off like a steam train, dust billowing up behind him as his hooves found purchase in the loose ground of the yards. We all watched spellbound as the distance narrowed between the two-ton enraged bull and the calm manager who was still walking unaware of the sharp and painful death that was about to hit him in the rear.

'Look out, Bob!!' Barry yelled, breaking the spell.

Without turning, the manager threw the notebook into the air and took off so fast he nearly dug a hole with his feet — the bull was only inches away from his back.

Even upmarket managers must have guardian angels. He shot up the rails like a goanna up a tree. For a moment it looked like he would fall back onto the bull as it crashed into the rails below with an almighty bang and a sharp crack. While the manager clung to the top rail the old bull collapsed back on to his haunches, then toppled sideways into the bulldust of the yard, dead.

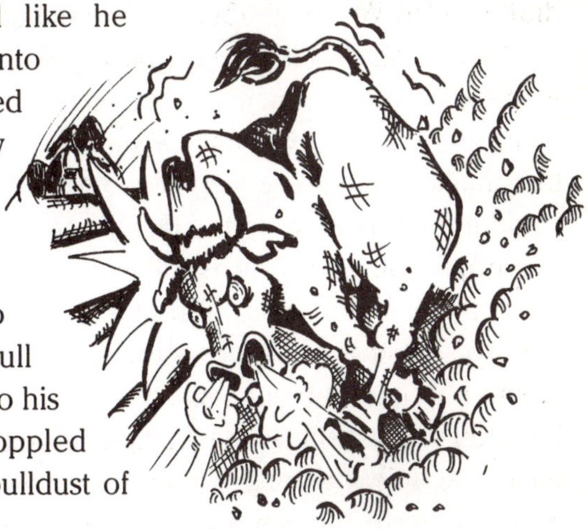

We all sat stunned as the manager climbed over to the head stockman, who was looking pleased with himself for having saved the man's life. I don't think any of us could believe the next few words the manager said to him:

'When you address me in front of the men, kindly use my surname. You are to address me as Mr Scandred, not Bob.'

Big Red

I was in Cloncurry getting an ear infection seen to and I was staying at the Oasis snake pit. This was a large room on the ground floor of the pub, separate from the main hotel. You threw your swag down on the floor and that was your space. The snake pit was a cheap place to sleep but you could get trodden or fallen on by the drunks coming to bed during the night. When the room was full of ringers, the air smelt about the same as if you had put your head into a sour beer barrel. Add to that the smell of unwashed clothing and it became hard to breathe, let alone sleep.

Much to my disgust, the doctor said that I had to stay in town and have daily dressings for at least two weeks.

A couple of the blokes that I met in the pub were talking about the amount of money they were being paid to drive old overloaded semitrailers to the new Mary Kathleen Mine where uranium was going to be mined. They were talking about the road being a bastard, how the loads shifted after the creek crossings and, on the last part of the trip, the big red hill. I told them that I had nothing to do during the day because I only had to have the dressings changed once a day.

'Come over to the rail yard tomorrow. The boss'll pay you to load the trucks.'

The next morning found me over at the railway yards

looking for the boss. He put me with a group of workers loading boxes and tying down the load. It was tough work and the beer went down easily at night, and the pay was more than I had ever earned before. Because I could drive they had me backing and driving these monsters all around the yard and outside to hand over to the drivers. (I didn't tell them I'd never driven anything larger than a two-ton truck. I had got my licence by driving the policeman out to the airport and back. At Mr Scandred's insistence they had given me a truck licence because I lived a long way from town and in an emergency I would have to drive any vehicle that was available.) At night the drivers took me through the de-clutching that was needed to change gears. I never thought that at 16 I would be doing this sort of thing. It was a long way from the Sydney suburbs.

I arrived at work one day and the boss said, 'Doc, I'm one driver short, the bastard's still pissed. The pay's 50 pounds a load. Take the Ford but remember you're overloaded by seven tons so you have 20 tons on board. The brakes are only good for a short time so it's down through the gears — and for Christ's sake don't miss a gear. You saw what happened to the rig that didn't make the bend.'

I was excited but at the same time I was shit-scared, so I said, 'Okay, no worries, I'll take it easy.'

I drove the rig down the main street feeling as if I was king of the road. I pulled up at the pub and had a beer with Slim, the driver, who looked terrible.

'The road's not bad but take it easy. When you go through a patch of windy road try to build up as much speed as you can and hold your hand down on the horn — that's to let them know on the big red hill you're on your way. The bloody hill is a bastard, you'll have to go down through your gears as you climb. Look out for parts of loads that have come off trucks before you. And you mightn't make the top with that heap of shit. So when you come to a stop, keep the motor running and don't let the rig go backwards down the hill. If you feel it going, take it sideways and jackknife it.

Don't worry,' he said as he saw the look of horror on my face, 'they've got workers with wedges placed on the hill, so stop as close to them as you can. They'll hook the 'dozer on to you and pull you up to the unloading area. Have a good trip, mate,' he said as he ordered another beer.

For the first time in my life I was worried that I had bitten off more than I could chew.

'Bloody hell. What the hell, I'll do it,' I was thinking to myself as I climbed up into the cabin. I started the motor and then tried to put it into first gear.

Ggggggrrrrrrrrrrrr! I was having trouble. I think I reminded myself, 'Let the revs die and hold the gear lever against the gate.' Clunk, in it went and I was away.

Driving wasn't too bad once I had the rig rolling but the amount of gear changing was making my leg sore. A few times the creek banks nearly beat me and the trucks that had left earlier and were returning empty gave me a fright as they came barrelling out of nowhere, missing me by inches because I couldn't move over with the load on. It was hard enough keeping the overloaded semi on the road. The road — if you could call it that — was dirt and very narrow, and with all the dust hanging in the air the visibility was nil.

I was on the windy road and crossing a stony ridge when a truck that was coming from the opposite direction blared its horn and the driver signalled me to stop. I stopped right next to him.

'G'day, Doc. I didn't know you were driving, I thought it was Slim.' We talked for a while. 'You have a mile of this,' he said. 'Then you have to take some chances and build up some speed. Get that heap of shit going, the mob on the hill is expecting you. See you back at the 'Curry.'

I drove along, making sure there was nothing that could fall on the floor and get under the pedals. Then I started to rev the hell out of the truck and slowly build up speed, holding my hand on the horn whenever I could. I moved fast around a corner with the tail sliding, corrected past a Landrover that had pulled off the road, then down the windy track and my first view of the hill. Jesus! It was a mile high. I was worried and the road was so rough that I was flying around the cabin.

The truck hit the bottom of the hill and we started to climb. Down through the gears I went. I was halfway up and I could feel that the load had shifted because the steering was light. Ahead there was gear strewn all over the road and as I came upon the drums and boxes I had to weave in between them. This caused the truck to lose more forward speed. I was now down to the last gear and the engine was starting to labour — I wasn't going to make the top. I looked around for the workers who were supposed to be on the hill. I couldn't see them.

Suddenly they were alongside the truck. 'We're ready when you are, just sound your horn and stand on that brake,' one of them shouted at me. I nodded and thought 'now or never', braked and sounded the horn. 'Stay on the brake, we'll have you hooked to the 'dozer in a sec, mate.' I looked up ahead and saw that I had nearly made the top. The 'dozer was coming down as fast as possible with a large chain.

After hooking me up, the 'dozer driver called over to me, 'I'll take up the slack, then you gun the motor and I'll start to pull the truck up to the top. Give me a hand by driving your rig.'

On the way back I nearly lost control and crashed into a creek because I was travelling too fast and was overconfident without a load.

I made a few more runs out to the mine but the station manager was getting his knickers in a knot and wanted me back at work.

The End of an Era

There was a new Willeys ute waiting in the railway yards for me to deliver out to the station. The manager had been waiting for it for months. I went around and picked it up. It was great, the first new vehicle I had ever driven.

So I went back to the hotel and picked up my swag. I had quite a few beers in the bar, then set out to beat the record to Quamby. I drove like a man possessed over grids, airborne down through creek crossings and over plains. I was flying. I roared into Quamby with minutes to spare for the record. I was so pleased with myself that I sat around drinking beer and nips of OP rum. I knew I was getting drunk when I caught myself talking to myself in the toilet, so I rang the station and told the manager that I was on my way.

'You sound drunk, Doc. Should you drive? I don't want anything to happen to that ute, I've been waiting months for it.'

'No, I'm okay. See you soon.' I hung up and went back to the bar for another rum.

The publican and the barman tried to talk me into having a sleep and driving out later.

'No, I'm right,' I said as I staggered out to the ute. 'See you on the next trip.'

I was so drunk I was mumbling to myself but with the wind coming through the window I thought I would be all right to drive. I roared out of Quamby and up the hills at the back of town. I was driving fast, enjoying the feel of the dirt road and handling the ute through the corners. I was out of the climb and about six miles from Quamby, travelling through spinifex, huge ant nests and some scrubby trees. The road surface was gravelly and dusty, and the ute's rear was breaking away on the corners.

It was coming into one of these corners that my life came unstuck. I came into it too fast and braked too hard. Instead of letting the ute spin I tried to drive it through. That was my big mistake. The front wheels hit a rut and the next thing I knew I was airborne, off the road and swinging the wheel to miss the anthills. I thought I could drive it back onto the road, so with a yahoo I jammed my foot to the floor.

Oh no, there was a tree in front of me. Smaaash! A branch speared through the passenger side windscreen. I twisted the wheel away, trying to miss the tree and realised I still had my foot on the accelerator. Whack! The branch sheared off the roof and with a huge BANG I took the tree out and then careered across a small clearing, clinging white-knuckled to the twisted steering wheel. I was yelling at the top of my voice, 'Stop, for Christ's sake, STOP!' and with that powerful command the ute ploughed into a ten-foot-high ant nest that brought it to a sudden halt.

Looking around, I found the cabin now housed the motor. The force of the collision with the tree and the ant nest had driven it through the fire wall. I turned the motor off and checked myself out. Except for a few cuts and bruises and a shoulder that I could hardly move, I was all right. I tried to get out but the door was jammed, so I pulled myself through the driver's side window. I walked over to an ant nest and sank down to the ground. I put my head between my legs for some time and then, when I thought I could face it, I looked at the ute.

It was a wreck. There wasn't a panel on the whole vehicle that wasn't dented beyond repair. From the front to the back everything was broken and the roof looked as if someone had used a blunt can-opener to make it into a convertible. The body was at least a foot shorter. The manager was going to sack me.

Suddenly I heard a horn from the road. I looked over and found it was the mailman. He stopped by the side of the road and in a few seconds he was with me.

'Christ almighty, Doc, you certainly know how to wreck a vehicle. You all right, mate?'

'Yes, but I don't know what the boss is going to say, he's been waiting months for the delivery of this ute,' I said as I stood up and dusted myself off.

'Don't worry, we'll think of something. In the meantime I'll back in and we'll tie this wreck onto the bar at the back of my truck and tow it into Quamby. It's only about five miles and I don't think we can do any more damage.'

So we attached the ute's rear onto the bull bar, lashed the steering wheel and dragged the wreck back to Quamby. On the way we got our story right. The mailman had seen a mob of cows break from cover and he'd seen me swerve to miss them. That's how it all happened. And this had all happened a few miles further on, where there was an old creek bed, not on the flat country where it had really happened.

When we arrived back at the hotel they all came out to see the sight. There were many knowing shakes of the head and the publican told me to tell Mr Scandred that I hadn't been drinking.

So I went in and rang him.

'Doc, where are you? You're long overdue and we are all worried.' (And he did, to my relief, really sound worried.)

'I'm at Quamby. I've had a bit of trouble with the ute.'

'What kind of trouble?'

'Oh, I had to swerve off the road to miss a few cows.'

'Is there any damage?' Now he sounded unhappy.

'Some.'

'Front or back?' He sounded short.

'Yes.'

'What do you mean, yes? Well, come on, tell me the worst.' He sounded angry.

'Well, I think it's a write-off,' I said very loudly into the phone.

'A what? How can you write off a ute missing a few cows?' He sounded very angry.

I started to tell him the damage and the phone line started to break up, with the help of the ringers at the bar.

This was a party line and everyone was listening in. The line wasn't good at the best of times and a trick we all used if we had bad news for the boss was to hold the mouthpiece away from our mouths to make it sound, with all the background noise, as if the line was breaking up. I had my arm stretched right out!

'This line is breaking up,' said Mr Scandred. 'I'll come in tomorrow and pick you up, but if I find you've been drinking, you can pack your bags. Okay?' he roared through the phone.

'No, I haven't.'

'Okay, see you tomorrow after breakfast.'

Click. We all stuck together and until this day Mr Scandred never knew the real story, but it was touch and go the next morning.

For punishment he had me chipping weeds around the homestead and buildings for three weeks — I found muscles in my back that I never knew existed.

The Day Mother's Face Fell Off

Whilst I was on Granada, Mr Scandred and his wife extended an invitation to my mother to come up for a few weeks and see what life on a cattle station was about. Now, my mother was a Sydney North Shore matron of some social standing who was used to ringing tradesmen and shops and expecting to get immediate service. I didn't think that she would fit in amongst the dust, flies and heat.

But I did want her to come and see me, so I wrote to her anyway and asked her if she would come up and visit me. I bet her that she wouldn't come and it was a happy surprise for me when I received an answer a month later, saying she would come and asking what was the best time. Mr Scandred told me the best time would be after all the cattle work was finished for the year and before the wet, so a date was picked in November.

I was so excited. By this time I had been away from home for two years and I was still a bit homesick. When the time came to go into Cloncurry to meet the TAA flight, I was even more excited and wished that the Ford ute could get there faster.

The road from Granada was just two tracks of bulldust which got into everything. So on our trips to town we always stopped at Quamby, had a drink at the pub to wash the dust away and asked if anyone wanted anything from town. Sometimes there were stockmen who had let their horses go in the Quamby Common and stored their gear at the pub and they wanted a lift into town.

We stopped in, picked up an order from some drovers, had a OP rum and beer chaser and hit the road to the 'Curry. We arrived early, so I went around town with Mr Scandred while he did some business and then to the managers' and owners' pub, the Courthouse, where it was seen and not heard for me while the bosses talked.

Then it was the moment I had been waiting for, into the ute and out to the airport to meet my mother. We arrived at the airport and got out of the ute, it was the middle of the day and the searing, dry heat was overpowering. At the airport there was a small building which only opened when a flight was due, so most of us were standing around where the plane would park, talking to the passengers who were heading out.

A faint buzz and a flash of silver in the cloudless blue sky, and there was the DC3 coming out of the east. She was flying low, so we got a good look at her as she circled before floating down and landing. As the plane travelled along the runway it shimmered and at times seemed to disappear within the heat waves above the tarmac.

The bloke from the stock and station agency directed the plane in with two wooden bats and when the engines had stopped he pushed the stairs into place.

I was standing under the wing as the pilot came down the stairs and he nearly had a heart attack when he caught sight of me.

'Hey, put that bloody cigarette out, do you want us all to go up in smoke?' he yelled at me.

There I was, under the wing, smoking away, trying to look like a grown up man of the world — with hot engines and fuel just above my head. I was hastily putting out the cigarette when Mr Scandred asked, 'Is that your mother at the top of the stairs?.'

I looked up and there was Mother. She looked as if she was going to afternoon tea at the Hotel Australia. I was so proud of her. She was dressed to kill in a beige linen suit and a large wide-brimmed hat from June Millinery, and she had a light tan bag which matched her high-heeled shoes — and, of course, the gloves.

'Yes, that's my mother.'

As I watched her stand at the top of the stairs and look around, I almost burst with pride. Seeing me, she gave a regal wave and made her way down the stairs to where I was standing. I gave her a big hug and a kiss. The heat on the tarmac was scorching as it radiated off the surface.

I introduced Mother to Mr Scandred and then, as we walked back to the ute, her face fell off. Well, not quite literally, but cracks started to appear in the foundation that she had plastered on her face and once that had happened the whole of her make-up started to landslide.

Luckily, Mother had lots of handkerchiefs in her handbag, which she went for. It was too late for damage control — the make-up had hit her chin and was running down her neck. We looked on with horror because we didn't know what to do but, without losing stride, Mother wiped her face off. So we went, full of admiration, to retrieve her bags from the car trailer which was used to bring the bags from the plane to the airport building.

Mr Scandred had decided that the hotels in Cloncurry were too rough for Mother, so we stopped at the milk bar in the main street. There she had a chance to dive into the ladies' room and try to put her face back on again. We had a goat's milk shake each, then it was into the ute and off out of town.

Mother chattered on about the family and home, looking out the windows at the passing parade of wildlife. I had lived in the Gulf Country for two years by this time and I suddenly realised that I had been taking the birds and animals for granted. With her enthusiasm and delight, Mother made me see them again.

Flocks of green grass parrots flew up from the long grass, and pink and grey galahs screeched as we disturbed them. In the trees near waterholes were corellas and white cockatoos, plains turkeys dashed across the road, along one fence a mob of emus were racing the ute and, high in the sky, kite hawks circled endlessly. The kangaroos that we had been cursing on the way in now became things of beauty as Mother sat looking excitedly out of the windows of the ute.

We stopped at Quamby for a drink, which Mother needed by this time, and she had a thirst-quenching beer instead of her normal sherry.

It was after this stop that a smell that had been worrying us started to get worse. It was a funny metallic ammonia smell and it was getting so bad that we had to open the windows. Poor Mother, it wasn't her day — her linen suit was smelling worse than an old sandshoe. It was so bad that we had to stop the car in a stand of timber to let Mother change into something else. She was very embarrassed and couldn't apologise enough. We worked out that the smell was caused by the chemical used by the dry cleaner when he had cleaned her suit.

From the tone of Mother's voice when she spoke of the cleaner, I would have hated to be in his shoes when she confronted him on her return.

We arrived at the station and unloaded the ute. I took Mother in and introduced her to the residents of the station and walked her around to show her my quarters and introduce her to my mate John Bennett and the other jackaroo.

The station came alive with Mother around. I was told to keep clean and to change my clothes daily. Usually, since we worked from early morning until late, we only had to wash our face and hands when we were eating at the manager's house. Now the manager's dining room was full because our neighbours came to dinner to listen to Mother talk about fashion and the happenings in the big city.

Mother Lost the Will to Speak

A few days after Mother's arrival, Mr Scandred told us at dinner to go out early the next morning and round up and bring in a few killers to the paddock near the river. He would come out in the Rover and kill one of the animals. Mother excitedly asked if she could come out with him since she had never seen a bush killing. After some attempts at discouraging her, he finally agreed but firmly said she had to stay in the truck. John and I rode out early, found the cattle without any trouble and slowly drove them to the place where we were to meet Mr Scandred.

The Rover arrived and I could hear Mother talking like a threshing machine. The truck was parked a little way off and as Mr Scandred climbed up into a nearby tree, we herded the cattle in under it.

Crackkkkkk! A shot rang out and Mother stopped in mid-sentence as the killer hit the ground with a crash and John turned the other cattle away.

'Stay with your mother. I'll get these cattle out the gate and into the other paddock.'

I nodded and jumped off my horse, tied him to a dead branch, jogged across to the truck, grabbed a butcher's knife and ran in to cut the animal's throat and start the bleeding procedure. Mother had climbed out of the truck but on seeing what I was doing quietly climbed back in. I don't think I have ever seen my mother as lost for words as she was then.

But soon, as we were cutting up the carcass, she was out of the truck, asking questions and talking to all the boys as if they were long-lost friends. We cut up the carcass and while John and I rode back slowly to the station, the others hopped in the truck. We were happy to ride back, since they would have to salt down the meat and none of us liked that job.

We Could Have Danced All Night

Barry, John and I were hanging around the station waiting to go on holidays. In the meantime we were causing trouble with the cook's daughter and the housemaids. We knew the wet was nearly upon us by looking at the dark clouds that were forming on the horizon and we didn't want to be caught out because we had our fares booked on the TAA flight out of Cloncurry in eight days and if we were too far from the station we could be trapped for a month.

Mother was still staying at the station when Jim Mitchell and Jack Ward arrived at the jackaroo quarters very late one night. They were on their way home from Cloncurry and they had three bottles of bush OP rum with them. John and I got up but Barry, the head stockman, wouldn't join in as he was worried about Mr Scandred hearing us and coming over. We all got very drunk and I put on some rock 'n' roll because the boys all wanted to see the dance craze from the city. The party got wilder and wilder as the rum flowed but it calmed down quickly when two of us danced — or fell — through the glass doors on to the verandah. Jim and Jack helped to clean up the mess and wisely cleared out before sun-up.

In the morning Mr Scandred was down on us like a ton of bricks because we had woken the whole station with our noise. John and I wouldn't tell him who had called in, we just said it was a couple of stockmen on their way through. He knew how to find out, though. He sent for Barry and, using a small threat, soon found out that it was in fact the manager of Kamileroi Station who had called in.

The shit hit the fan. Mr Scandred was furious that Jim hadn't come to the main house and made his presence known because that was company law. The next thing we knew we were all summoned to the office. Mr Scandred had been on to head office demanding a full apology from Jim and he also wanted to dress us down. There was a no grog policy and he wanted us to admit that Jim had brought alcohol onto his station. Luckily Barry could not answer that as he had stayed in his room the whole time and so he hadn't actually seen anything. Jim knew we wouldn't tell but we were very worried as all our jobs were on the line for quite a few hours.

Mr Scandred was finally happy with an apology from us and from Jim and a promise that if anyone called in to the station, they would be sent to the main house before they called in on us. I got ticked off by Mother because she would have liked to join the party.

We were given terrible jobs around the homestead — cleaning out the chook yards and cutting down prickly bushes. We had worked out that we only had to keep clear of Mr Scandred and his wife until it was time to leave and then we would be home free. I had a worse time than the others because Mother was staying at the main house and I was expected to eat with the family but Mother came to my aid by chatting away and keeping the family entertained.

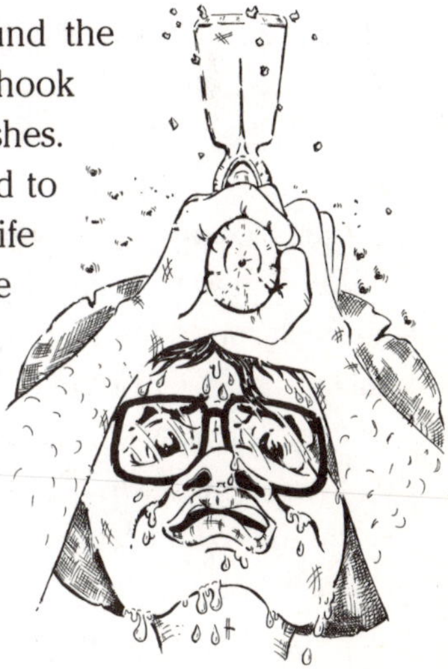

The Last Straw (Bore)

Mr Scandred and Barry were driving all over the station checking on the stock, fences and water. Late one afternoon Barry came looking for us to tell us that we were wanted at the office. He didn't look happy but Mr Scandred did, he was fairly beaming as he broke the news that we had been picked to go out and fix a broken-down windmill at the 40-mile bore. This windmill was on the bank of the Leichhardt River so when the wet hit there would be plenty of water for the stock and we could actually have gone out after the wet to fix it. But company policy stated that if a windmill broke down, it had to be mended in case a lot of cattle died if it wasn't fixed.

Of course this was just what Mr Scandred was looking for, a job to pay us back for what we had done to him. So no amount of complaining and pointing out that if it rained we could be caught out there for a month or more, or even through the whole wet, would change his mind. He just said that we were wasting time standing around arguing, when we could be getting out there and back and no, we couldn't bloody wait until the end of the wet.

With a lot of swearing we went and packed our swags, drove the Willeys ute down and hitched up the four-wheeled trailer. We loaded this with casing and rods, the tools, two fuel drums (one of diesel and the other petrol) and a 44-gallon drum of water. Then we went up to the cook to get some supplies.

We left the homestead late in the afternoon with Barry and me in the ute and John following driving the tractor. Every time we stopped to open a gate we would look westward to see what the sky was doing. It didn't look too bad but the track we were following ran parallel to the river and if rain fell up in the hills the water would cover the plain we were travelling over for miles. The country was made of deep black soil, clay pans and salt pans, and when wet the black soil became like bottomless treacle. So we were pushing both vehicles to their limit to get out there, fix the bore and return as soon as possible.

We arrived at the crossing — the bore was on the opposite side of the river to the station — and waited for John. We were pretty well set up with the four-wheel-drive ute, the big tractor and the huge four-wheeled trailer loaded with enough food to last us through the wet. We drove down the steep bank and across the dried up riverbed which was around 80 metres across with steep clay banks on either side.

While John and Barry started to organise the pulleys on the windmill's steel frame to pull up the rods, I set up camp. I emptied the ute and drove it back across the river and parked up on the other bank, so that if anything happened we had a vehicle on the right side of the river to make a dash for the station. I got the meal ready and we had the ropes and everything set up to start. After dinner we tried to work under the lights from the tractor, but after nearly having a bad accident when John's hand got caught under a length of casing we were lifting, we went to bed.

The next morning saw us up early, turning the windmill out of the wind and then unhooking the rods and hooking them up to a double pulley. The rope from that went up to another pulley fixed at the top of the windmill, then down through a block and out to the tractor. It was a bit tricky to start with — we had to raise and lower the rods using the tractor so that we could pick up the foot valve down below.

So with the tractor running forward and reversing, lifting and dropping, we turned the rods with pipe wrenches, trying to catch the thread. Once we had picked that up we started pulling up the rods. The rods were around five metres long and we had to undo them as we pulled them up, making sure that we secured the bottom rods as we unhooked them. Then we stacked these rods upright inside the windmill frame.

Now came the casing, which was a bigger job. The casing was heavier and we had to unscrew each length. It was too long to stand in the windmill frame, so we had to run them out on to the ground. We had around 30 rods and 20 lengths of casing.

It was a big job pulling the rods and then the casing up. We found that where the casing was screwed together the minerals in the water had nearly eaten through the joins, so they were hanging by a thread and we had to be very careful as we raised them. We knew they could break off and disappear into the hole, blocking the bore hundreds of feet below, and that would mean drilling another bore and replacing the windmill, which would cost a lot of money.

Working carefully but flat out, by late on the second afternoon we had nearly finished. We only had around five lengths of casing to pull up when disaster struck.

John was on the top of the windmill watching a huge black cloud coming towards us while he unscrewed the puller.

'Hey, there's a bloody great storm up at the head of the river. We'd better stop pulling the casing out and stick it all back down,' John yelled down to Barry.

'We have to finish or Scandred will go up us,' Barry yelled back.

'Well, you can bloody well do it on your own. I'm not getting caught out here for a month for anybody.' John yelled this as he clambered down the windmill frame.

I threw my two bob's worth in: 'I'm with John, let's get the hell out of here. Even if we start now it will be three or four hours before we finish.'

'Okay, let's do it,' yelled Barry, after a bit more verbal persuasion.

The light was fading as the black storm clouds built up around us. We were as worried as hell. Then an hour later the storm broke over us, we could hardly see in the downpour. I went and got the ute since it was quicker than the tractor for lowering the rods. We also had a better chance of getting back to the homestead on the tractor which was now facing the river with its diesel engine running and the trailer packed and hooked up.

In the downpour we were having trouble picking up the foot valve, a metal cylinder at the bottom of the rods which helps lift the water.

'Pull the rods up and drop them, that sometimes works,' I yelled to Barry as he backed away, pulling the rods up. After he had dropped them a few times and we still couldn't pick up the foot valve, he backed up as far as he could, lifting the rods right up the inside of the windmill frame to the top pulley. Then he drove forward fast. The rods came down like an express train and to our horror kept on going down as the clip holding them broke. The three of us stood in the pouring rain listening to the noise the rods and casings made as they disappeared into the bowels of the earth.

The thought that ran through all our minds was 'Mr Scandred will kill us!'.

Suddenly John was down the windmill, yelling, 'The river's coming, can't you hear it?'.

I ran to the tractor and gunned it for the riverbed, then Barry jumped on as we roared down across the river. We made it over the hundred metres of riverbed, but the tractor started to spin halfway up the steep bank on the other side. John had managed to unhook the ute and was right behind us in the riverbed.

'I'll unhook the trailer,' yelled Barry as he jumped down to the coupling. John was already there hooking the wire rope to the sling that we had attached to a large gum. The rope was wrapped around the power take-off on the side. I gunned the motor and without the trailer we inched slowly up the bank.

'Good God, look!' Barry yelled in my ear. Around the bend of the river came this huge wall of water, throwing trees and rubbish up in the air. It looked higher than we were but as it hit we topped the bank. Even so the water rose halfway up the tractor.

'What are we going to tell Mr Scandred?' Barry asked.

'Not we, you! You're the head stockman,' John and I said.

It was a long drive back to the homestead and none of us felt like talking. We were thinking we had buggered the bore, when last seen the ute was being flattened by a huge log and we had lost the trailer with all the tools aboard. Not bad for three blokes who were in the shit already.

As soon as we hit the station Barry went straight to the manager's office to break the good news. John and I went to the kitchen where we sat down nervously to a hot meal. While we sat eating, we could hear Mr Scandred bellowing over and over again.

'You lost what???'

'Where did you leave the ute???'

'The trailer is where???'

'Aren't you lucky you aren't the head stockman?' the cook said, grinning, as she brought in the sweets.

Into the Bottomless Pit

It had been raining and I was at the station to load supplies to take back to the mustering camp. I had come in the night before, expecting to go out again the next day. But the rain had come down in buckets all night and I had no chance of getting through the station horse paddock because it was black soil and bottomless. I had to wait for over a week before the rain stopped and the ground was hard enough for the Willeys and the large four-wheeled trailer loaded with supplies to plough their way through the mud.

The black soil in the station paddock had already claimed a victim — the bulldozer was off the road and had sunk to the top of the bonnet. It was going to stay there until after the rain had all gone and the soil dried out, which would take a month at least.

It was time to give it a go and head for the camp. The sun had been shining for two days and the ringers had been in touch and told us they were getting low on supplies.

'Stick to the road once you get out of the horse paddock. The clay pans will be okay but the black soil will build up under the mudguards and stop you,' Mr Scandred said as he saw me off.

I hit the road through the black soil and had a bastard of a time trying to keep on it. The trailer was everywhere, first out one side going sideways, then out the other. It was throwing the Willeys all over the road and I had to wrestle with the wheel to save the vehicle being speared off into the bottomless pit of black soil. We were coming up to the ramp sideways. I thought, 'this is it, we're going to hit sideways', but at the last minute the trailer straightened and we roared over the cattle grid.

The road outside the paddock was better and I made good time. By now I was in the clay pan country. There was some water on the surface but the clay itself was solid. I came around a corner and in front of me was a stretch of water with deep wheel tracks up to 50 feet long. Without thinking I looked to the side and since the ground looked solid I swung the wheel. The ground seemed to be all right as the ute and trailer left the track but when I turned to go back in a loop to the road we broke the surface and the vehicle started to sink.

I couldn't reverse because I had the trailer, so I had to go down through the gears and plough ahead. I thought I was going to make it but about ten feet from the clay pan the ute came to a spinning halt.

I turned the motor off and looked at the safe ground just a short distance away.

'Oh well, I'll have to dig myself out,' I said as I tried to open the door. The bloody door wouldn't open. Christ, how deep was I down? I crawled out of the driver's side window and surveyed the situation. It wasn't good. I had pushed a wave of black soil in front of me and the doors were half buried, and the trailer was down because it had been following in the ute's wheel tracks. Time for a smoke as I thought of how to get out of this fix.

It was too far either way to walk, so I had to get myself out. Lucky for me when we loaded the trailer we had loaded the winch and the axe. And there was one saving grace — I wouldn't starve.

I started to dig the front of the ute out so I could jack up the wheels and put branches under them. Doing this would help the wheels get some purchase. By nightfall I had it dug so that I could get the jack under, so I stopped and ate some tinned food and spread my swag on top of the trailer.

The next morning I was up early and after some tea and tinned food I set to with a will. I could get the jack under the wheels but the ground was bottomless and as soon as I tried to jack up the wheel the jack would disappear into the mud.

It was late afternoon before I unhooked the trailer and tried to get the ute out. By nightfall I had the ute on dry ground but I had to stop because the light was gone.

The next morning I ran out the winch. It was the type that you crank by hand. I hooked it all up and tried to winch the trailer out but I couldn't move it, so I spent the afternoon unloading the trailer and carrying the goods to higher ground along the road. I wasn't going to let it beat me and I didn't want to go back to the station and tell the manager I had gone off the road because I think he'd had about enough of me.

It was dark but I didn't want to spend another night there, so I made a fire so I could see what I was doing. It was around nine when the trailer came loose and I could crank it out. I hooked it up to the ute and drove up to the supplies.

I had just started to load them when a voice came out of the darkness — I nearly jumped out of my skin. John rode into the firelight.

'What in the hell have you been up to, Doc?' I looked down at myself, I looked as if I was made of mud — you couldn't see my clothes.

'I turned off the road and went down. I'm glad to see you.'

'We saw the fire that you lit, so I saddled up and rode back to see if you were all right,' John said as he dismounted and came over to give me a hand to load the trailer. 'The track from here is good — we didn't get as much rain as the station did.'

We loaded and I drove slowly through the night to the camp. They were pleased to see me because they were out of tobacco. I lay down as I was and slept — I was stuffed.

Young Love – or Lust

My move from Granada was in the wind. It happened after Mother's visit and about three months after my first trip back to Sydney, helped along by the only girl for 100 miles. On Granada we had a woman cook and her 16-year-old daughter was staying with her.

The cook and her daughter had a great time — well, the cook didn't because she was kept busy making sure that we didn't get too close to her daughter!

I was one of the lucky ones because I had set up a darkroom in the old kitchen in the jackaroos' quarters and the girl wanted to learn about photography. So every time she could get away from her mother we would go and do some darkroom work together. I must have been a good talker because I got her mother to let her meet us at the lunch camp. The only stipulation was that one of the women from the station had to be with us as her mother was worried about her daughter's reputation and her associating with another class. In those days working class people thought that the 'upper class' would play around and get their daughters up the duff, then piss off to marry someone from their own class.

At one stage a concerned Mr Scandred stepped in and barred her from coming to our quarters, and gave me a lecture on the facts of life.

'It wouldn't be in your best interests to get involved with this young girl. I know she is attractive but you are both too young and she really is below your station. Think of the scandal if she fell pregnant — it would be the end of you in the company.'

This only added fuel to the fire. We would sneak away whenever we got the opportunity. I had a great time and it eased the loneliness of being amongst men all the time without the softness and love of women.

Not only that, I was crazy about her. I would follow her around and when I was working she would look for me. One day I was helping build a tall shed for storing the bales of hay that we had cropped on the other side of the river. I was on the roof, spray-painting it red, when she came up the ladder, so I started to skylark and show off.

Whooooooosh! My feet went from underneath me and I started to slide down the roof over the red paint. I grabbed out to stop myself and clutched a handful of her dress instead. This not only pulled her over but also tore her cotton dress nearly off. In my other hand I still had the spray gun. I could feel the hose stretching but I thought it might slow me down.

Snap! The hose broke. I wrapped my arms around the girl to stop her being hurt when we hit the ground. With a scream from her we went off the roof into the air. But we didn't fall far because we hit the hay trailer which was half unloaded and then we rolled down the bales. On the way down, the spray gun broke and covered us in bright red paint. We ended up sprawled out among the bales, her with only her panties still on and me with my shorts half down and my shirt half torn off. Both of us were covered head to toe in paint — and of course the hay had stuck to us.

It was while we were in this situation, unsticking ourselves, that Mr Scandred came across us. He was lost for words but I could see my career flashing before his eyes. The wrecked ute, the lost bore, partying in my quarters and now having it away in the hay with the cook's daughter.

'I know it doesn't look good but I can . . .' I didn't think it was worth finishing. Here I was, standing on some bales of hay with my arm around this near-nude girl, holding her tight so she wouldn't fall off.

So Mr Scandred found the solution. He sent for me and said that I was being moved to a larger station, Kamileroi, because Jim Mitchell, the new manager there, had requested my transfer. I was happy since I had been hoping for this for a long time but it was the end of my romance. So it was with a heavy heart that I packed my bags and arranged for the horses I had bought to travel up to Kamileroi with a drover who was taking his plant past there when he went to pick up a mob at Lorraine Station, the next one past Kamileroi.

At the last minute Mr Scandred decided that the drover could take me with him to give him a hand with the horses. I was pleased because I loved seeing new country and what better way than from the back of a horse.

My departure day arrived. I was woken early, my gear was loaded onto the drover's truck and I was sent over to Mr Scandred's office to say goodbye to the cook and her daughter, who was returning to the safety of boarding school in Charters Towers. Mr Scandred, his wife and children, the ringers who were in at the station and the other jackaroo, John Bennett, were all there to see me off with handshakes and hugs as I saddled up and headed out to join the horse tailer. (John was also transferred to Kamileroi some time later and we worked together until I left the Gulf and returned to Sydney.)

Arrival at Kamileroi

The ride up with the drover and the rest of the boys was great. We rode all day. Then at dusk we would hobble the horses and come into camp, and after we ate dinner we would sit around the camp fire listening to tales of all the rides and rushes the drovers had done. It took around five days to get to the boundary of Kamileroi and while we were putting the horses through the gate a Ford customline ute came barrelling up the road, throwing dust out in every direction.

'Here's your new boss, he always drives like that,' the drover said as we sat on our horses waiting for the ute to arrive. I could see two people sitting in the front. When the ute came to a halt, the first person to throw open his door was the driver and that was Jim Mitchell.

'Hey, Doc, it's good to see you. Get down, I want to introduce you to John Steele, the number two camp head stockman.' I jumped off my horse and pumped Jim's hand because he had taught me all the bush lore and ways to behave I knew up 'til now.

John Steele was a tall young bloke in his early 20s and the first thing that he said to me was: 'I don't believe you're a jackaroo. You're the first one to turn up who can ride and you're not dressed in flat-heeled boots and a funny hat, arriving on the mail truck with a huge suitcase instead of a swag. If Jim hadn't told me you were coming with the drover's plant, I would have thought you were a drover or a ringer.'

'Thanks, John,' I said. It was a great compliment and I could see that we would get on.

'Doc, unsaddle your horse and let's go to the homestead and have a drink,' Jim said, as he went over to talk to the drover. 'They can drop your horses at the tank in the horse paddock with the others.'

'Okay, Jim, I'll just say goodbye.'

In a few minutes we were heading back to the homestead and another adventure had started.

The station homestead and the surrounding buildings, yards and vegetable gardens were around four or five times bigger than Granada. The homestead itself was a two-storey affair, very grand. It seemed like a dream come true, just to be finally there.

Hey, They're Shooting at Us

One of my most amazing adventures started when our camp was sent out late in the year to muster some cattle that were hanging on our western border. The manager, Jim Mitchell, thought they were a bit of a temptation to the small property holders in the hills. They could come down in the wet, take the cattle into the hills, change the brands on the cattle already done, and mark the cleanskins. If they did the branding in November, by the time we got around to mustering these stragglers in March the changed brands and the branded cleanskins would be healed up and we wouldn't be able to pick them out. The small property holders would happily come down to help with the first muster after the wet. We would campdraft 'their' cattle out of the mob so they could take 'their' (our) cattle home.

We drove the horses out to the camp and the next morning, with a few storms around, we set out to muster these cattle. We split up and spread out, mustering towards a waterhole where we would have lunch. Usually after lunch over half the camp would ride out and muster the other side of the waterhole while the others held the cattle already mustered at the waterhole. When we reached the waterhole at lunchtime we had only found the old bulls and weak cows. We couldn't find any of the 400 to 600 head that would normally be hanging in this area.

At the waterhole we came across some bush yards, which are temporary yards built with post, rails and logs, in order to hold the cattle for branding. This process is called bulldogging. The stockmen hold the cattle while a couple of riders rope and drag the animals to the rails or logs where the branding fire is burning. One man grabs the calf and throws it. Then the brander runs in and marks it with a brand. If it's a bull they castrate it, then let it up. The frightened animal jumps up, mooing loudly, and runs into the mob to find its mother.

The head stockman, John Steele, myself and a couple of the Aboriginal ringers, who were top trackers, checked out the camp.

'Boss, these cattle only left here about dawn this morning and the riders are driving the whole mob west. They wouldn't be at the boundary yet.'

I was shown the clues by the older Aboriginal ringer — fire coals still hot and cattle pads still soft and wet, and, of course, the unmistakable tracks heading off towards the west.

The head stockman said to the ringers who had gathered around him waiting for orders, 'Let's go and get these cattle before they disappear for good.'

The ringers talked amongst themselves. John, the Aboriginal stockmen and I were to one side so we couldn't hear what was said.

'Sorry, we can't do it. We aren't being paid to chase cattle duffers,' said Terry, the horse breaker, who was acting for the mob.

John nearly went off his head. 'If you don't do as I say, then you'll all be put off when we get back to the station.'

It didn't make any difference to these riders because they could always get other riding jobs.

At last it was decided that they would stay at the waterhole and wait. We would send one of the boys back when we got the cattle and they could ride out and give us a hand to get the cattle back to the yards.

So we set out. John Steele, myself, the two trackers and the boy who would ride back as soon as we got the cattle.

We made good time since the tracks were in damp ground and hard to miss, and we took a short cut across a mile or so of erosion which they would have had to take the cattle around.

As we came out of the erosion one of the trackers pointed to the base of the hills. We could just make out the black dots of cattle and riders starting up one of the valleys between the hills.

'I'll give them warning. They'll scatter when they see us coming.' As he said this John flicked out his stockwhip and started to crack it.

You could see they had heard us for they started to rush back and forth, cracking their whips to make the cattle move faster.

'Come on you bastards, let's get 'em!' John yelled as he kicked his horse into a gallop. I was a bit slow and the trackers were a lot slower as the words of the other ringers came back to them: 'You aren't getting paid to risk your neck for a mob of bloody company cattle.'

'John, two of them are riding our way,' I yelled as I caught up with him.

Crackkkkk! Crackkkkk! Puuuuuuuuuu! Puuuuuuuuuu!

'Hey, those bastards are shooting at us!' I yelled in fright.

'Hold up,' shouted John as he pulled his horse to a halt. I pulled up with him. The boys were about 50 metres behind.

Crackkkkkk! Crackkkkkkk! And dust rose on either side of us as the bullets ricocheted off the ground and into the air.

'Back to that clump of gidgee, fast!' John yelled as he spun his horse and galloped for the nearest cover back the way we had come.

Crackkkkkkkk! The sound of another bullet flying past made me spur the horse — I was riding in a flat gallop. We reined up in the trees and looked back. The horsemen had got the cattle moving fast and they had passed our boundary markers and

were disappearing fast into the hills.

I have never seen John so angry.

'Those stupid bastards shot at us! They actually fired at us, they're mad. We'll get them, whatever it takes.' John was pulling his horse around in anger. 'Come on, let's get back to the others.'

Walking our horses back to where we had left the other ringers was too slow for John.

'I'm going to ride ahead to the others and swap my horse for one of the spelled ones. Then I'll ride to the camp and raise Jim at the station on the wireless. I think he should go after them. You take your time getting back to the camp — I don't want all the horses knocked up.'

'Okay. See you back at camp,' I called to John's back as he cantered off to the camp.

When we all arrived at the camp John told us to make ourselves comfortable because Jim was on his way. He was coming out with a police tracker in the morning.

The next morning I was up early to get the horses. The night horse had been tied up all night since there were no paddocks and the other horses were all in hobbles. They hadn't moved far, so I just had to walk around them and push them together and then the ringers could walk out and catch their mounts for the day.

By the time we had had something to eat, Jim had arrived with a policeman and a tracker from Dobbyn. We caught and saddled horses for them and headed out in the late morning. We took a spare horse and a pack horse with some rations, driven by one of the boys. There were six of us: Jim Mitchell, John Steele, the policeman, myself, a tracker and the horse tailer. We made good time until we came to the hard country, where there had been a heavy shower overnight. Because the light was failing and we didn't want to come upon the riders in the dark, we stopped and camped in a hollow without a fire, so that no-one would see us.

The next morning we started off early and searched for tracks but by lunchtime, except for a couple of old cows, we hadn't seen or heard any cattle.

The tracker and the horse tailer weren't trying too hard and I couldn't blame them as they weren't being paid enough to risk their lives. Mind you, neither was I!

Jim could see this, so after an hour he said to the tracker, 'You, Doc and the horse tailer wait here while we scout ahead and see if we can find any tracks or cattle. Do you have any idea which gully they would have taken?'

The tracker pointed to one of the gullies that headed straight into the hills and while Jim and John Steele changed horses we found a bit of shade to sit under and wait for their return.

It was just about dark when they came back and said we would camp here for the night. We could have a fire, for by now the bush telegraph had told everyone that the police had left Kajabbi and were on Kamileroi looking for some poddy dodgers.

Sitting around the fire the policeman said that they had seen a rider on one of the far hills, but by the time they had found a way around the gully that was between them the rider had long gone and it was getting too dark to follow the tracks. We went to bed in our swags and were awakened by a heavy shower just before dawn. So the morning light found us crouched around a small fire trying to get warm and dry out.

'I don't think there is much use trying to follow the tracks today, this rain would have washed them away. What do you think?' Jim asked as he looked at us around the fire. The tracker and the policeman agreed and as it was my first time I shut up.

'Okay, we'll go back today but I want you to tell me when any of those stations in the hills bring cattle in to Dobbyn to rail out to market,' Jim said to the police officer.

'That's okay by me. Let's ride.'

We all went back to camp and packed up and then the whole camp moved back to the station because the wet was due to start any time. I was put in the station garage to help the mechanic. I had been on this job for two weeks when Jim came down and told me to get ready because we would be going into Dobbyn early the next morning. The police had rung to say there was a mob of cattle coming in from the hills and they felt we should look at them since it was late in the season to send cattle out.

The next morning saw myself, Jack Ward, the head stockman of the other camp, and two ringers heading into town with Jim in the Landrover. We met Charlie Brown, the mailman for the Dobbyn to Burketown run, on the road and he told us that the town was waiting to see the fireworks when we hit town.

'How did they know we were coming? We were only told yesterday afternoon,' said Jim. 'We were hoping to surprise them.'

'Come on, Jimmy,' said Charlie. 'You should know better than that. The bush telegraph is alive and well — and don't forget that the town likes the hill mob more than the company-run station people. They come to town more and are related to a lot of people in the district. Why don't you just turn around and forget it? They're only company cattle after all.' It was possibly the longest speech Charlie had ever made.

Jim shook his head. 'No, I can't do that and you know it. Anyway, we had better get going. We don't want to keep the town waiting. We'll see you later in the week, Charlie.'

With that we drove off into town. In the car the ringers, Jim and the head stockman were discussing what would happen if the hill mob caused any trouble. Jim said that if anyone threw a punch or looked like causing trouble we were all to move back and let the police handle it.

The ringers were a lot happier when this was decided, since most stockmen in the outback have a soft spot for battlers and one day they might want work from them. Besides, stealing from the large company estates was always happening. Most station, drovers' and camp killers were strangers and the odd poddy dodging was always on, but there was some honour — horses and equipment would be left untouched, no matter how long you left them unattended.

Dobbyn was a small settlement at the end of the rail, surrounded by a large common or fenced area. It consisted of a few houses, a police station, a railway station, cattle yards and, of course, the pub, which wasn't much, just a single-storey building with hitching rails out the front. The whole town was dusty because all the roads were bulldust. When there were cattle yarded the dust rose and if the wind was right it blew right over the town — plus the added bonus of the smell.

As we approached the town from the north we could see that there was a large mob in the yards and the hitching rail in front of the pub was full of horses.

'We'll go straight to the police station and see what's happening,' Jim said to all of us and we quickly agreed, as none of us wanted to go to the pub and get into a fight. We drove through town to the police station. Jim thought it best if we waited by the car so he could go in and find out what was going on.

It wasn't long before he returned with the two policemen.

'The police here have stopped the loading for about two hours but the train has to leave this afternoon or we'll have to pay for its delay. So we have only a short time to put some of the mob up the crush and check for any brands that have been changed with a running iron, or branded over. So let's get down to the yards and get into it.'

We climbed back into the Rover and headed to the yards. It seemed that everyone in the district was down there. If they weren't standing around the yards in amongst the cattle they were sitting on the rails. There were women and children too and they were having a great time laughing, chattering and playing around.

It seemed that the cattle were a mixed mob from three of the holdings in the hills. The owners' names escape me now but one of them had a very small holding and yet he seemed to have a lot of good cattle to send to market each year. He was the one Jim aimed all his remarks at when we met them outside the yard. This bloke was young and good-looking and had grown up in the district, so he was well liked.

'Okay, Jim, the police have stopped us from loading for two hours so you can look over some of our cattle. My friends are here to see that you'll have your job cut out to inspect too many of them.' And with a sweep of his arm, he said to Jim with a big smile on his face, 'My friends have come to enjoy the show.'

I could see Jim was having second thoughts about doing what we'd come to do but his face hardened and he turned to the police. 'What are you going to do?'

'We're here to keep the peace and we'll arrest anyone that starts any violence, so both of you blokes better tell your mobs that.'

Turning to Jim, he continued, 'We can't help you to crush these cattle because there's no evidence they're stolen but if you find any we will take in the person in charge and question him.'

'Okay, let's go, and take no notice of the hecklers on the rails,' Jim said as he made his way to the gate of the inner yard.

We moved into the large outer yard and started to push the cattle towards the smaller yards leading to the crush — and that's when the fun started. Every time we got the cattle up to the gate someone would casually jump down from the rails and walk across in front of them, sending them back on top of us. If we looked like beating him the people perched on the yard rails would wave their hats and yell, pushing the cattle back upon us. This went on and on. It was becoming a circus and the locals were having a great time. They had even carried one of those half drum BBQs down and were handing out steak sandwiches.

We got about ten head of cattle up to the crush and found in amongst these a cow with a new brand that looked as if a running iron had been used — and it was missing the ear that should carry the ear mark. Another cow had what looked like our brand under a new brand and an ear that was freshly marked. We ran these two into a small holding yard but by now we had run out of time. The train driver came and told us he was going to get the train loaded. Jim went over to talk to the police while the whole town helped load the train — fast.

The police said they would hold the cattle we had drafted out in the common and get the cattle inspector to look them over and give a report. They would take the bloke who supposedly owned them up to the station and get a statement from him now. We stood by and watched the mob being loaded, and when it was finished the townspeople retired to the pub while the police escorted a very angry bloke to the police station.

We were still standing down by the yards when a yell went up from the pub and everyone piled out on to the road to see what the commotion was all about. Running down from the police station with his chaps flying in every direction was the bloke who had been taken in for questioning. One of the policemen had taken up the chase but he gave up in the first 50 yards and headed back to the police station for the car. One of the ringers in the pub had the bloke's horse saddled and was holding it ready in front of the pub. The bloke came running up and jumped into the saddle and, with a roar from the pub crowd to urge him on, he took off across the common at a flat gallop.

The police Landrover came down the road like a bat out of hell, swung off the road and started to gain on the horse and rider. Just as they caught up with him he veered away and sent his horse at a wide erosion. The horse took it beautifully with a cheer from the crowd — we even gave a small shout at the show of horsemanship. The police vehicle didn't jump — the driver tried to turn away but the car skidded sideways out of sight in a large cloud of dust.

'Come on, we'd better make sure they're all right,' Jim yelled as we all piled into the Rover. When we got there about ten horsemen were standing around the two policemen, who were knocking the dust off themselves.

'He got away. We'll get him after the wet when he comes into town for supplies and after we get the cattle inspector's report we'll see what we can book him with,' one of the policemen said.

Their car was still upright down the side of the erosion and with everyone's help and with our Rover we soon had it back on level ground. We all retired to the pub but just before going in I noticed a tiny little speck moving up into the hills.

Jim explained that the reason he had done all this was because he was a new manager and he wanted to give notice not to take him lightly. It seemed that everyone agreed and after we'd been to the pub we drove onto the common, unrolled our swags and slept until the sun woke us. The trip home was silent, since we all had big hangovers.

Six months later, after the wet, the two cows in the common had disappeared. There had been a big BBQ at the pub at Christmas and without this evidence the police couldn't do anything. As for the bloke who took off on them, they just gave him a talking to. But after that Jim didn't have as much trouble with the mob in the hills.

One Dog, One Owner

One of the most important things in the outback is water and making sure it is always available. This is the job of the boundary riders and the windmill experts. The boundary rider lives on his own with his dogs and horses, miles out in small huts set up at bores or at waterholes where large mobs of cattle water. His job is to check and repair boundary fences where there are any, keep an eye on yards to make sure cattle don't get caught in them, and check and repair the fences of the night paddock and holding paddock.

But the boundary rider's main duty is to check the bores and waterholes in his area, once a week if possible. He checks to see that the cattle are actually getting to the water in the waterholes and not bogging in the mud if the waterhole starts to dry up, and makes sure the windmills and bores are working so cattle can get water.

He reports by radio to the station weekly or, in the case of a breakdown, straightaway. The other thing he watches out for is the condition of the stock and any suspicious tracks or movement of cattle.

The windmill expert works in with him, checking bores, windmills and turkey nests (mounds built to hold the bore water). He cleans out troughs and renews worn pieces of equipment. Sometimes, if there hasn't been any wind to turn the windmill, some of the bores require diesel motors to help the flow. Especially if big mobs are watering there during the dry season, these motors have to be checked every few days to make sure they have fuel and haven't broken down.

The first time I came in contact with one of the old school of boundary riders was when a woman and her husband were being shown around the station by the manager and I was taken along to open the gates (it always seemed as if there were thousands of the bloody things).

We arrived at the boundary rider's cottage. The manager had told the couple this boundary rider bred a special type of cattle dog.

'These dogs work in pairs and are called nose and tail dogs,' he explained. 'When an animal breaks from the mob the ringers are trying to yard up, the boundary rider will let these dogs go. They race after the galloping animal, one grabs its tail and hangs on, while the other dog latches on to its chin or close to the head and hangs on too. With the beast moving at top speed and throwing its head around trying to dislodge the dog on its head, the dog on the tail swings out the other way, throwing the animal to the ground.'

We did the same thing from our horses. We would gallop up behind an animal, grab his tail and then, holding the tail, kick our horse to overtake the animal. This would pull him off balance and down he would go. Most times when the animal regained his feet he had had enough. A few cracks of the whip and he was heading back into the mob.

The manager explained further, 'These working dogs mustn't be touched by anyone except the person who works them, because if the dogs answer to anyone else's call, they could get killed in the yards or when they work cattle out in the open. Some of the owners use severe penalties for a dog that takes any notice of somebody else and for the people that handle or call them, so be warned,' he said to both the visitors. The old man we were visiting was one of the best breeders and trainers in the Gulf and his dogs were his life. Dogs were not generally used by the Australian Estates stations, except when yarding on some stations.

When we got there we all piled out and walked around to stretch our muscles and to get rid of some of the dust. The old bloke appeared from around the back where you could hear dogs barking. One command from him and they all shut up.

We had some billy tea that was so strong you could stand a spoon in it. I think it had been brewing on the side of the stove for a day or so. The old man was of medium height with longish grey hair and a brown, weather-beaten face that had more wrinkles than a prune. He was wearing old patched grey riding trousers and an old faded khaki shirt with the sleeves rolled down, and his hands were covered with old torn cloth. (If you worked on fencing in the cold dry season or if you knocked your hands, the skin would break open and take forever to heal because you kept knocking the sores open all the time. The main thing to watch out for was Barcoo rot, an infection that ate down into your flesh. A lot of the older ringers had it badly all through the colder times of the year.)

While the manager was talking the couple went out of the hut, I thought to the Landrover. I stayed to listen to the old man's reports. When he had finished we walked out onto the verandah, where we saw to our horror that the woman was nursing one of the pups and talking to it. The old man spun around with a strangled cry and rushed into the hut.

'Come on, Doc. It's time to move.'

The manager and I ran down, grabbed the puppy from the woman and dropped it on the ground, then bundled the couple into the Rover.

'What's the matter?' they both yelled at us, sounding a little frightened.

'I warned you not to touch another man's dog,' the manager yelled. 'Didn't I?'

The couple could only nod their heads.

'Well, that old bloke takes the bush rules seriously. I'm afraid he might snap and shoot at us, some of these boundary riders are a bit strange, living like hermits year in and year out.' While he was talking fast the manager had started the four-wheel drive and he'd got it moving by the time the old man came out of the hut.

I had to jump out to open the house paddock gate only about a hundred yards away and while I was holding the gate open for the car I saw, through the dust, the old man shakily trying to load the rifle as he walked up to the puppy. Then I heard the crack of the report as he shot it. I had the gate closed and was back in the Rover in record time.

It was a very quiet group that headed back to the station. But I must say, I have seen fights in the yards when ringers have called out to other men's dogs, and I've also seen a few working dogs kicked and trampled to death by standing looking confused when two people called commands out to them in the yards. It takes years to train good dogs, so you can't afford to lose them.

I'll Have Mine with Tomato Sauce

One of the main jobs of the boundary rider is to report any windmill breaking down so the mustering camp can send a group of riders to muster the cattle watering there and move them while the windmill gets fixed. Sometimes he lets the camp know too late and by the time we arrive there are hundreds of dead and dying cattle in and around the troughs.

I was in the station store buying a few bottles of cordial when the manager came rushing in.

'The boundary rider has just let me know that the windmill out in the north-western corner has broken down and the cattle have been hanging there for a week. So there are a lot of dead cattle to drag away and a lot to be moved before they die too. I'm trying to get the windmill expert but he is working on another bore out the other way, so I'll have to drive out and get him,' he said as he moved out of the store.

'Doc, grab four of the ringers, they're down at the fuel depot moving drums around. Get them to pick up their swags and some chains, and get the cook to pack you a few days of food. By that time the camp should be out there to move the cattle. See if there is anything you can do to fix the bore but the main thing is moving the dead cattle away from the water.'

By late afternoon we had arrived out at the bore. We found that the rods had broken, so there was nothing we could do to fix it. There was a little water for us in the bottom of the turkey nest to cook with and drink but not enough to wash in.

The cattle were hanging around because they could smell the small amount of water. It wasn't a nice place to be. You could taste the smell of rotting flesh and I think every fly in Australia was there, they were all over us. And the noise was terrible. Above us the air was black with circling kite hawks and there must have been 20 dingoes lurking. A couple of hundred head of cattle lay dead and bloated all around the two long water troughs and at least another 500 were staggering around mooing. We camped inside the fence of the turkey nest so the cattle wouldn't walk over us in their desperate search for water.

After a bad night's sleep because of the dingoes howling in our ears and the cries of the cattle we were up before dawn. We had brought two vehicles — one truck and one Landrover. We split up. One vehicle was to work around each of the troughs with long chains hanging off the back tow bar and the front bull bar. We had decided to drag the carcasses over to a deep erosion about 200 yards away and try to roll them in. I was shown how to wrap the chain around the animals' legs so the vehicle could pull them away.

Everything was going all right in the cool hours of early morning but as the sun rose and the air became hot and dry the carcasses started to swell to twice their normal size. All around were these huge round brown barrels with four legs pointed stiffly into the air. I had just stepped back from wrapping the chain around this very large bloated steer when the driver yelled, 'It doesn't seem to be holding, Doc. Can you take a look?'

I quickly moved in to look at the chain since it looked okay to me. As I bent over to check I heard the motor of the vehicle roar and the chain snapped tight as the vehicle jumped forward.

Booom! Poooffff!

The carcass exploded and as the air escaped from within it so did all the smelly bits and pieces.

I was covered in this dripping shit from head to foot. Luckily I had a piece of cloth covering my mouth and nose and my hat was low on my forehead, so most of the muck missed my face, but it was plastered all over the rest of me. The front of my clothes looked as if I'd been hit by a family-sized pizza.

'I'll kill the bastard! I'll kill you! Look at me, I'm covered in shit.'

I only stood for a second or two before I took off after the Landrover and what spurred me on to catch it was the laughter coming from the front seat. It took two of the ringers to grab me and stop me from hitting the driver but none of them could stop laughing.

I had a hard time seeing the funny side of it, for without any water to wash in I might have to stay like this for a week.

I used dust and grass to wipe off the bigger pieces of muck and try to clean myself down. And now I found thousands more flies loved me. I swore I would get even with that bastard.

That afternoon the rest of the camp arrived and started to move the poor dying cattle to another water. The windmill expert and his offsider arrived and started to work on the windmill. I couldn't help myself, every chance I got I went over to the windmill expert and asked him how long before it was pumping again, because I wouldn't mind a wash. My clothes were stiff by now.

We kept on moving the carcasses. All of us were pretty dirty and smelly but no-one smelt as bad as me, and to find me you only had to look for the cloud of flies with riding boots sticking out the bottom. The other ringers who were out to move the live cattle made us sit downwind from them.

In the afternoon the carcasses were blowing up without any interference on our part. It was getting to be touch and go who would be the next one to get covered. Then it was my turn to drive and the ringer who had got me earlier in the day was putting the chain on. I tried a number of times to get him but he was too quick to jump back. I thought that I would never get him.

But then he must have slipped. When I looked back there he was, lying over a large old cow. This was my chance. I jammed my foot down on the accelerator and shot forward. As the cow exploded the ringer was thrown into the air in a wet green cloud of shit and cow guts. I didn't stop. I headed to the gully with what was left of the carcass, laughing my head off.

This job went on for three days without us being able to wash because the windmill expert had to send to town for some parts. On the third day the company grader arrived and started to push the carcasses into the hole and shove a lot of dirt over the top.

I think the worst thing wasn't the smell but the flies. There were blowflies and black bush flies. The blowies stayed with the carcasses but the bush flies were all over you. They were in your eyes, they were in your ears and if you didn't have the cloth over your mouth and nose they were in both those openings too. It was at this time I heard the sayings 'Do you know why outback people talk without opening their mouths?' 'Why?' 'So the flies can't get in!!' and 'You can always tell a city bloke, he's always choking on flies.'

We finished moving the carcasses from around the troughs, though there were still a lot around in the nearby scrub. The windmill was fixed and the expert had run a hose down from the turkey nest for us to wash under. We stripped off and hosed each other down. We must have washed for over an hour to get rid of the smell.

This job was one we thanked heaven didn't occur very often. And when it did you tried not to be found when the manager or head stockman started to look for men to go out and clean up.

Hold Me, Don't Ever Let Me Go

The whole camp was riding out to muster early one morning. We had a long ride before we could muster back to the waterhole that had been picked out to hold the cattle on. Riding out were two old Aboriginal trackers, about eight ringers, John Steele (the head stockman) and myself. The trackers were having a great time pulling the bark off trees as they were riding past to get the witchetty grubs. The cattle pad we were following wound through the white box and river gums so the grubs were plentiful. To eat them when they were riding along, they used to hold the grub to their mouths and bite off the head, then put the grub, headless end first, into their mouths and with their fingers pull it back out, squeezing the insides out by using their front teeth. They said it tasted a little like peanut butter. After a lot of persuasion I tried some and I agreed that the taste was similar — it was the mouthful of moving soft hotness that worried me, but like everything you get used to it.

We were riding along laughing and joking. I had the trackers tell me about the tracks in the bulldust and what they thought, by looking at the tracks, the reptile, bird or animal had been doing. Then they would ask me what I thought some of the tracks were and sometimes I would get one right.

One of the things the ringers loved to do whenever they saw a snake, and if they had a bit of time on their hands, was to jump off their horse and run after the snake, grab it by the tail and swing it around their heads. (Some of the bigger snakes seemed to come back halfway along their own bodies, which I thought was pretty scary as they would angrily writhe around in front of your face.) Then when the ringer was ready, he would crack it down on the ground the same way as cracking a stockwhip. This meant the by now cranky snake came down only inches from your ear. I had no trouble swinging them around my head but I couldn't bring them down past my ear. I would swing the snake around in a circle and then let the bastard go, so it flew through the air and landed a long way away from me. If you cracked a snake right its head would fly off, if you didn't you had one hell of an angry snake at your feet.

The day was starting to heat up, one of the black ringers jumped off and cracked a snake then hung the carcass in the fork of a tree to pick it up on the way back.

'Hey, Doc, the next snake is yours,' the ringers yelled with lots of laughter, knowing how I felt about handling them. I hated the feel of snakes so I was not happy with the thought of grabbing one by the tail. I rode along hoping that we wouldn't see any.

'Look, Doc, over there, a big silver one, go get it.'

I looked over to my right and there, going around a bush, was the tail of a large snake. I jumped off my horse, hooked the reins around a fallen branch and ran over to the snake. The ground rose up behind the bush and by the time I arrived the snake was heading down a hole. There was still about three feet of its tail visible, so I grabbed hold and pulled. The snake had felt me grab him and seemed to be hanging on, I couldn't pull him from the hole no matter how hard I tried. It was at this time that I realized that something was waving across my face. I looked up ...

F...k!!! I was looking into the eyes of a snake which was about six inches from my face. In my panic I started to let the tail go but the more I let it go the closer the snake's head came to my face.

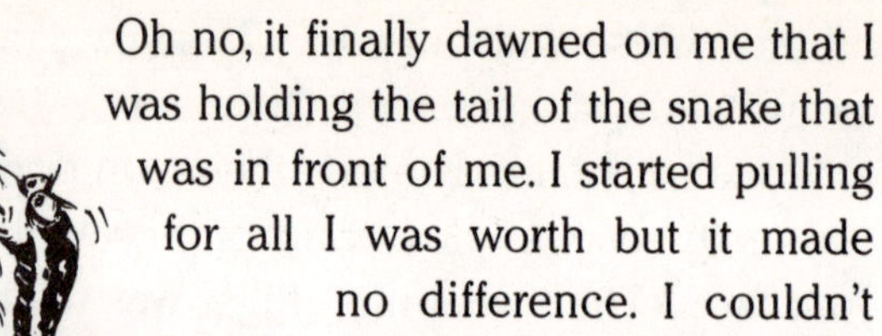

Oh no, it finally dawned on me that I was holding the tail of the snake that was in front of me. I started pulling for all I was worth but it made no difference. I couldn't move the bastard. We were at a stalemate.

'Hey, can someone help me. This snake's got me, I can't let him go.'

Suddenly a horse and rider came crashing by and I could hear the other horses snorting and jumping around and the ringers swearing and shouting. One ringer on his horse came up behind me and warned, 'Doc, get back on your horse, the place is alive with snakes. We must have ridden onto a nest of them. Come on, stop hanging around.'

I went to say something then I noticed that the snake was in a crack that ran right to my feet. It was only a matter of time before he would have me and I had no idea how poisonous he was.

Whooooosh. A stirrup-iron flew past my shoulder and hit the snake's head. As the snake went down, I let go of the tail and jumped back. Next to me was one of the trackers swinging his stirrup-iron and smiling. As I scrambled away I could see snake tracks everywhere in the soft dust.

'Come on you lot stop mucking around we have work to do. Doc, that's not much of an example to set to the ringers, running around chasing snakes,' the head stockman yelled at me as I remounted.

On the way back to camp the black ringers had collected the snakes they had killed and hung in the trees. That night they came up from their camp with a pile of cooked snake for us.

All That Dough

Cooks are the unsung heroes of the bush. This hardy breed of lunatics have everything to contend with, from trying to make something edible from nothing, flies, heat and meat going off, to the loneliness of getting up early to cook before dawn and then being on their own all day in the camp.

There are two main groups of station cooks — those who are always at the homestead cooking for the manager and the men working around the station, and the camp cooks who travel around cooking in the mustering camps. The camp cooks were always men and sometimes the station cook was a woman, but this was rare because the people running the stations in those days thought that women were too much trouble to have around and tried not to have them working on their stations.

I must admit that women in those days had it rough. I can remember one particular roo shooter who travelled around in a caravan with his wife and always camped miles out in the scrub away from the mustering camp, because he was worried about the ringers getting on to his missus. He was a top shot and we were all warned to stay clear of his camp but some of the ringers took it as a challenge.

Here was this poor woman, stuck for months at a time cooking, reloading ammunition and dressing hides, with no-one to talk to. It wasn't any wonder that when the shooter brought her into the mustering camp to pick up supplies and mail she wanted to talk to us. He used to get jealous and take her away from there as quickly as possible.

Bush cooks were notorious for their heavy drinking. But these men couldn't touch the demon drink on the stations for months on end, since all the stations had a 'no drink' policy and if you were caught bringing grog to the station it was instant dismissal. Sometimes you would see a ute load of ringers on their way home stopped in the shade of some trees, finishing off the grog they had bought for the trip out of town because they couldn't take it onto the station.

It was a sorry lot that turned up back at the station after a week in the 'Curry. The manager would send them out to the mustering camp the next day so they could sober up. Some of the older ringers would hide this amazing OP rum which was like treacle — you had to add water or you would die. I don't know what proof the stuff was but it could remove varnish and was great for pouring on wounds. In hotels and at the rodeos I have seen it being used for sterilising cuts and abrasions.

Anyway, these old blokes would secretly carry a bottle in their saddlebag until we were mustering and as soon as they were out of sight of the head stockman they would drink it straight from the bottle. It was around 100 degrees in the shade and we wouldn't be getting to water until lunchtime, so it was a superhuman effort for them to stay in their saddles and muster.

The horses seemed to know if the drunken ringer was going to fall off. If he was toppling, the horse would move to catch him. The horses looked as if they were doing tricks, weaving and jumping in all directions. At lunch camp we would make sure the head stockman didn't see the drunks. While he was having lunch we would keep them on the other side of the mob and when he went back out to the mob one way we would take the drunks into the lunch camp round the other way. It was only for a few days before the bottle or two they had brought out would be finished.

Sometimes the manager would send us out to set up camp as soon as we arrived from town and keep the head stockman in the homestead for a few days to go over the mustering plans. Then a party would take place out at the camp. Some of the ringers, drunk on rum, would muster the horses in and we would have a rodeo, with ringers trying to ride horses they couldn't ride well when sober. There would be horses bucking everywhere. It was lucky that no-one was badly hurt. There were lots of cuts and sprains but by the time the head stockman arrived all the grog was gone and the camp was very subdued and ready for work.

There were other ways to get grog onto the station. The mailman was a great source. He would hide it in the load and you paid him in town, so you wouldn't be seen giving him money — not that any of us had money on the station. The only way we knew we were making money was a statement of earnings that was given to us every month. This statement would have the goods that you had bought from the station store deducted from it. Most of us only bought tobacco, papers, matches, soap, toothpaste and cordial (to drink at camps where there was only bore water, most of it was only just drinkable with cordial or as tea, never straight).

The other way to get grog was through the cook. If you got on with the cook he would let you into his supply. It was pretty heavy stuff. As you are possibly aware, cooking essences are made up with alcohol as their base. Another grog recipe contained boot polish, with potato peel and dried fruit left to soak and ferment.

When I first arrived on Kamileroi I nearly got killed. I was left in the camp to help the cook with bread making and whilst he was sleeping I came across all these covered camp ovens with a foul-smelling, evil-looking watery mess in the bottom. I threw the lot out, washed and scrubbed the camp ovens and placed them on the table to dry. I was down at the waterhole getting two buckets of water when I heard this almighty yell.

'I'll kill him, the bastard! Where are you, you mongrel?' I could hear the cook shouting at the top of his voice. I thought he was in trouble with a snake or something, so I dropped the buckets and ran for the camp. As I came in view I could see the cook running around the camp with a huge butcher's knife.

'I'll kill him!'

He looked up and saw me and started to charge. 'You bastard! I'll kill you.'

I didn't know what he was going on about but he was running at me with a very large sharp knife, so without asking him what his problem was I took off back to the waterhole. I could hear the cook pounding down the track and as he had a running start I knew that he was catching up to me. The fear of the sharp knife, one that would shave the hairs off your arm, being buried in my back made my legs move. Halfway down the bank I heard the swish of the knife at my back. Without waiting I launched myself in a flat racing dive into the waterhole. I hit the water and didn't stop until I was in the middle. Then I turned and looked back at the cook, who was standing on the edge waving the knife and swearing at me.

I carried on a conversation while treading water.

'What in hell's wrong with you, you stupid bastard? You could have killed me,' I yelled at him.

'What's wrong with me? You've destroyed my grog supply, you BASTARD.'

'What are you talking about?'

Then he told me that the stuff in the camp ovens was fermenting and he made grog from it, adding a bit of lemon essence to it for flavour. I told him I hadn't known what it was and I thought I was helping him by cleaning them out.

He turned and went back to the camp. I swam to the other side of the waterhole and stayed there until I heard the cattle coming into the yards. Then I went to the horse yards and saddled up and went out to help yard up.

I didn't tell anyone about it but I made sure that I kept out of the cook's reach for the next week or so. By that time he had another lot going, so he was happy again.

Once when the cook went on a bender I was elected to cook, so I moved my swag into the cook's tent and took over the portable metal-framed bed that cooks always get. This was luxury — a bed! The idea of the tent was so that the cook could sleep during the afternoon because he started around four in the morning to cook breakfast, wake the horse tailer, turn on the milking program on the radio — much to the annoyance of some of the lighter sleepers — and get everything ready for the day.

I was up and at it early, first waking the horse tailer, then cooking a camp oven full of porridge and making up powdered milk warmed by the fire. On this particular morning we had just killed the night before so there was fresh meat and liver to cook as steaks, and, of course, tinned butter (which had always melted and separated) to spread on damper toast with plum or melon and lemon jam.

After preparing breakfast I set out the lunch makings on the table so the ringers could make their lunches. This was normally two slabs of damper with jam one end and the meat of the day at the other. They wrapped it in newspaper for something to read at dinner camp. Then I had to bang a kero drum, once for the first call to wake up, and then around 15 minutes later to signal it was time to eat.

When they had all finished breakfast I washed up, checked the fire and had the first sit-down and smoke of the day. Since the fire was going and there were lots of coals, I floured a couple of camp ovens and halved the damper dough into them. Next, taking a shovel, I lined the bottom of the two holes in the ground that had been dug to fit the camp oven. Then I placed the ovens in the hole on top of the bed of coals and covered the lids with more coals. It would take the bread around an hour to cook, so I carted some water from the waterhole, checked the carbide lamps and made sure that everything that might attract ants or flies was put away out of their reach.

Then I threw myself down with a book on the cook's bed. With the heat I soon started daydreaming and fell asleep. I don't know what woke me but I came out of a dream with the feeling that something was in the tent with me. I lay still and opened my eyes.

'Jesus!' I yelled. I was looking into the eyes of a goanna, only a tongue length away from my face, standing on his back legs and looking into my face.

Craaaassshhhh!

I went out of the tent backwards as fast as I could, rolled under the side panel and came up running, only to hit the guy ropes, which tripped me. I only lay flat for a second, then I was up and off. But because I was looking back for the goanna and not watching where I was going, suddenly I was airborne.

'Oh no!'

I only had time to yell as I crashed to the bottom of the garbage hole. I didn't feel anything broken, so I stood up, wiping some of the muck off me. I climbed out, covered in all manner of garbage.

Looking around, I spotted the goanna sitting over in the shade. I could have killed him but now I was up and wide awake, so I grabbed my washing gear and went down to the waterhole for a swim.

Gelding a young colt.

Skinning a 'roo for the skin to make bags.

Cutting out on the camp face, a time for showing off horses and riders.

Looking down at the Gulf from a TAA DC3. The haze in the background is a dust storm rising to 3000 feet.

Burketown from the TAA DC3 Friday fish plane. The corridor between the seats was covered with huge frozen barramundi.

The bush radio — our only link to the outside world and the Royal Flying Doctor Service.

The Blitz truck that carried our gear and was used for fire fighting (note the ship's tank on the ground on the left).

Kamileroi's water supply.

Me cutting out a calf from the mob of cattle.

Windmill, turkey nest and water trough — the main source of water in the Gulf.

One of the special breed of nose and tail dogs.

Horse tailing — bringing in the horses to be drafted before going out mustering in the early morning.

Using the calf cradle to brand and mark calves.

Butchering — the skin is pulled back so the meat isn't on the ground.

The rib roast and the brisket being removed.

Bleached bones of cattle we had pulled away from broken down windmills.

The sky filled with kite hawks as we dragged the dead cattle away.

I gained a lot of cooking skills from the cooks in the bush. There were the times when I helped them, and other times when the cook went to town and I did it all by myself.

One cook at Kamileroi, Mick Nugent was his name, was one of the best cooks I have ever met. He was in demand with all the stations at the time I was there. He cooked in Jack Ward's mustering camp and when both camps were working from the station, he cooked at the men's kitchen in the station.

Mick had one problem — drink. He would be all right for about two months, then the lemon essence and boot polish order from the station store would double or triple. The manager would be told by the bookkeeper to get ready for the loss of one cook.

Mick would go and get drunk but the food would never vary. I came in for breakfast early one morning and couldn't see him but I could hear these loud snoring noises coming from the kitchen. As I walked into the kitchen I couldn't see a soul around but could still hear the snoring. I came around the big kitchen table and looked down. There on the floor was the large galvanised washing tub with what looked like a huge mound of white bread rising to a height of three feet and flowing down the sides of the tub. I walked around this mountain of dough and came across two legs with boots on, sticking out from the centre — and from underneath I could hear the snoring.

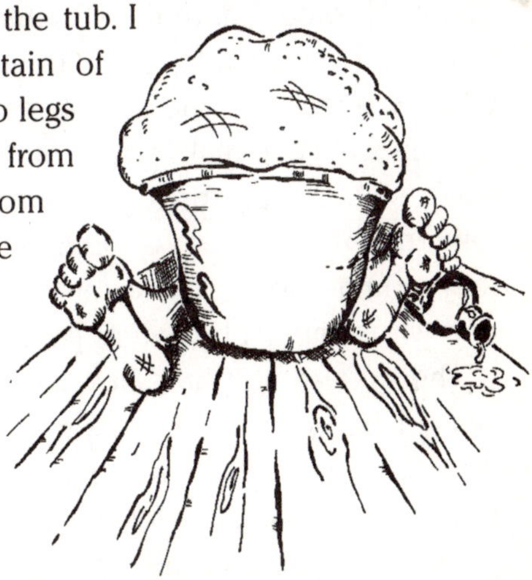

'Hey, you blokes, give me a hand. The cook's passed out in the bread dough,' I called to some of the ringers who had come into the dining room. I started to extract him from the dough but it took three of us to get him out onto the floor.

When he came to, he raced up to the manager's office, snatched his time and asked for his cheque.

The manager would play the game and if the mailman wasn't coming that day, Mick would demand that a light plane be ordered for him from the 'Curry, saying he didn't want to be on this station where everyone was against him.

The manager would order the plane and ring the publican at the Royal and tell him to accept Mick and ring him when the cheque ran out. What Mick and many other bush workers did was to get into town, go around to one of the cheapest hotels, give the publican their cheque and tell the publican to let them know when they had drunk the cheque out. This got them instant drinking friends, so three months' work lasted two weeks at the most.

Then, even if the cook had left the station calling the manager all sorts of a bastard, the manager would send one of us in to pick him up. We would throw him and his swag into the back of the ute and bring him back to the station.

Mick had another problem when he arrived back at the station. He would have the DTs and become very religious. No one could swear in his dining room or kitchen, or for that matter within earshot. If he heard you, he would come at you with a kitchen knife and make you apologise to God. There were times when some of the ringers wanted to hit him but they were reminded that he was a good cook and if they made him leave they would have to cook until the station could find another one, who wouldn't be half as good.

The other thing that Mick did as soon as he arrived back from a bender was go to the kitchen pantry and lock his guardian angels away. Yes, angels! Here was a rough and tough knockabout bush cook locking his angels up because he didn't want them to see him in the state he was in — and you were under the threat of death if you went near the pantry door. If Mick saw you near that door he would throw whatever he had in his hands — boiling water, hot fat, knives or bowls — so most of the ringers wouldn't go into the kitchen until Mick had settled down.

On Granada Station we had a camp cook named Bert. He was a short, fat old man who had terrible asthma as well as a drinking problem. The two combined were a deadly mixture. We used to ask him why he drank if he had these terrible bouts of asthma which nearly killed him. He would say that it didn't matter if he died because life wasn't worth living.

He was a good-hearted soul until the grog got to him. Then he would go off on a tirade about any little thing that went wrong. On our days off he would boil water so we could have a hot bath.

When he was on a bender in town he had a beer in one hand and his asthma spray in the other. Sometimes he would go black before he could get his breath back, which used to frighten the other drinkers a lot.

When it was time to pick him up from the hotel after the money ran out he would be unconscious and breathing with difficulty. As he couldn't open gates he would lie in the back in amongst the load and we would check him at every gate to make sure that he was still breathing. On one of these trips when we got to the camp we discovered that Bert was dead. He had had an asthma attack while unconscious and carked it.

Face to Face

I had always been a good swimmer and in the bush I felt like a champion because hardly anyone living on the properties in the Gulf Country ever got a chance to swim.

We had yarded 2000 head of cattle and had been drafting, branding and cutting them for two days. On the morning of the third day we started to let out mobs of 200 to 300 to go down to water. It was a narrow holding paddock, so most of us were riding out in front of the cattle, cracking our whips at them to slow them down, because after nearly three days in the yard without water, the cattle wanted to gallop down into the waterhole. We had to keep them at a walk or the poorer ones would get trampled and drowned. After they had been watered we had to turn them back and drive them out to where we had mustered them from. The first mobs were cows and calves so we had to hold them for some time while the mothers found their calves.

The last out were the bullocks. We had to keep these in the holding paddock so that the drovers could pick them up. There were around 600 head in the mob and when they left the yard they just swept us out from in front of them in their rush to get to the water. Most of the first bullocks to the water went in up to their shoulders so the others behind could drink. A few tried for their freedom across the waterhole but turned back when they came to the oil drums that were floating with wire tied to them. But one big bullock decided that he wanted to go all the way.

'Go get him, Doc. Show us how well you can swim,' the head stockman yelled.

I jumped off my horse, quickly stripped off, ran down the slippery bank and waded through the mud until I could shallow-dive into the milk chocolate water. From where I had gone in I was on an angle to the bullock, who hadn't seen me, so I thought I could easily cut him off. I swam into position and thought I would give him a big surprise. I would dive under the water and come up facing him, give a big shout and frighten the hell out of him. This would send him back to the bank.

I duck-dived underwater and swam for a point about ten feet in front of the bullock. I could hear him but I couldn't see anything because the water was like white coffee. I turned underwater to face him and rose to the surface. I opened my eyes and got ready to yell — and got the shock of my life! There, about an inch from my face, was the snout of a crocodile.

I let out a bellow that would have woken the dead. The croc headed for the far bank and disappeared with a mighty splash. The bullock must have done a tumble turn — I lost sight of him in my panic to swim back to the bank. As I hit the mud in the shallows and tried to swim up the bank I ventured a look back to see where the bullock was. I found I had beaten the bastard out of the water by a full body length. One of the ringers got a photo of the scene but the crocodile had gone before he could click the shutter.

There were quite a few freshwater crocodiles in the waterholes around Kamileroi. Most of the time we wouldn't see them, they sat on the bottom of the waterholes while we were around, for they were very shy. Our only fear was treading on them in the muddy water. A few of the ringers had been bitten like that.

The saltwater monsters were further down river in the tidal waters of the Gulf and they were definitely not to be messed with. A bite from a saltie would usually prove fatal.

Once, while riding home in the late afternoon, our horses became upset and hard to handle. We discovered the reason — a large saltwater croc was moving through the long grass. He was miles from any water. His hole must have dried up and he was crossing the plain in the late afternoon, heading for the river.

Pigs, foals and calves were often taken by crocs further down the river. They would simply put their heads down for a drink and disappear under the water, sometimes with a brief fight, so we didn't take chances swimming in any of the holes at the northern end of the property.

We had a mob of horses in our camp from further up into the Gulf Country. They had been reared there and were very cautious about drinking from any waterhole. The horses wouldn't stop close to the water, they would stand well away and stretch their necks as far as possible to just touch the water with their noses. At the slightest noise or movement they would take off. A lot of the more seasoned riders would get off and stand next to their horses, so if the horse tried to take off they could pull it around with the reins.

Let me tell you some of the crazy pranks we ringers would play on each other when we were mustering on other properties.

We would be mustering a dry area that was only fed by bores, so the only water in the area was in long troughs. This water was always hot and the water at some of the bores would make your mouth feel dryer even after you had drunk enough of it to make your stomach ache. One of the best ways to keep your mouth from drying out was to suck on a stone. We would arrive at a trough hot, tired and thirsty. Some ringers would dismount and the others, being too tired, would stay mounted. As the horses lent forward and stretched out their necks as if drinking from a river . . .

Sppllaaaaasshhh! — some smart arse would throw a rock into the water trough and with that the horses would fly backwards, leaving the rider sitting in midair without a horse under him. Others would end up on the horse's neck and they would slowly slide around and hit the dust. A few lucky ones would stay seated as the horse pigrooted around in fright. It was a circus, horses going in all directions, dragging riders around on the ends of the long red hide split reins, for if your horse got away you would have to walk home and that could be six miles or more. At night, talking about it made us all laugh but as it was happening we could have killed the bastard who threw the stone.

Speed Swimming

I had my closest encounter with a crocodile further up north. I was getting into the OP rum at the Burketown pub in the Gulf of Carpentaria. Burketown consisted of a pub and a few houses situated on the banks of the Albert River. The river was full of barramundi and huge saltwater crocodiles.

A couple of ringers and I had brought a mob of horses up from Kamileroi and were waiting for the new owners to come in and pick them up from us. We were drinking with a large crowd of blokes and as the night wore on the stories got bigger and better. Of course I felt I was in safe water telling stories about my swimming and sailing experiences.

Suddenly a large bloke jumped up.

'If you think you're so good I've got just the boy to beat you,' he bellowed so the whole bar could hear him.

'I'll take him on, any time, any place,' I yelled with drunken bravado.

Out of nowhere a bookie appeared and everyone started to place bets. I noticed that the locals were all betting on the local lad and they had me at 50 to one.

I started to sober up.

'Okay, here's what you have to do. You dive into the river with a rope attached to your foot and swim down and place the rope around an object on the bottom. The one to get his body back into the boat the quickest wins. It's as easy as falling off a log,' the large bloke said with a laugh that the locals joined in on.

'That sounds easy enough. When do you want to do it?' I looked around at the sea of smiling faces with a sudden feeling of apprehension.

'You said any place, any time, so I pick right now and right there,' he said, pointing out the door towards the Albert River.

'Hey, it's nearly midnight and the river is full of crocs,' I found myself yelling in fright.

'That makes it about right. Come on.'

All the drinkers trooped out of the pub and down to the bridge where the crocodile hunter had his boat. Yes, that's right. I now found out that the bastard was a crocodile hunter. He made his living killing and skinning crocs.

We clambered aboard the 18 foot clinker with its old Perkins diesel. On board were three blokes as referees, the shooter and a very tall Torres Strait Islander called Sunshine. I didn't have much time to talk to him as the shooter was explaining the rules or the lack of them.

'We drift down the river and I spotlight a croc and shoot it. Then you dive over the side, swim down with a rope looped around your leg, attach the rope to the croc, then swim back to the boat. We'll time you and the one with the fastest time wins. Okay?'

'Sunshine will go first to show you how.'

I looked over at a smiling Sunshine and saw where his nickname came from. In the dark all I could see were teeth, bright, shiny teeth. I wished I hadn't thought of teeth.

Boom!!!!!!!!!

The spotlight had picked up the eyes of a huge croc and the hunter had shot it. Sunshine dived over the side before the croc had stopped thrashing. The next thing he was back, clambering over the gunwale.

'Five seconds,' yelled the time keepers.

The others on board pulled the rope in. On the end was a monster that seemed to be all teeth. They lashed the carcass to the side of the boat and unhooked the rope from around its leg.

'You're up, Doc.' I stood poised on the side of the boat watching the spotlight, shaking like a leaf. It seemed to have turned cold all of a sudden.

Suddenly there was the glint of red eyes caught in the light.

Boom!!!!!!!!!

I felt a hand push the middle of my back, so I had no choice but to dive in the direction of the thrashing croc.

Splash!

As the black water cut off all vision I started to swim down, thinking my time was up. My groping hand struck something — a leg! I hoped that it was a back one, since I had visions of sticking my head down a croc's throat. I slipped the rope off my leg and put the loop over its claws, pulled it tight and then turned and shot to the surface faster than a speeding bullet. The side of the boat was right in front of me. I didn't even touch the sides of the gunwale. Suddenly I was in the boat, standing up.

'Eight seconds.' It was the longest eight seconds of my life and I wasn't about to call for a rerun. I shook hands with Sunshine and found to my horror that this was what he did for a living, earning just a few pounds a month. He said I was the fastest he had come across.

I think I downed about half a bottle of OP before the shaking stopped.

I Want to Lay Down My Head and Rest

In the Gulf of Carpentaria and in the Channel Country, when the summer dry grass and the electric storms were all around us, fires used to rage unchecked for days on end. We kept an eye on them and sometimes the station would have a plane sent out from Cloncurry or the Isa to check out the extent of the area being burnt. It was only when good grassland and homesteads were threatened that all the people on the station and adjoining camps and stations would move into action.

We couldn't fight the fires with water because the distances were too great and it was mostly unavailable. Our firefighting tools out at the mustering camp were an old flamethrower, diesel-soaked rags tied to poles, greenhide beaters, axes, fire rakes and wet bags. There was a large ship's tank of water on the Blitz truck with a petrol motor that was used to wet down the bags and we sometimes got the use of the company grader if it was working on the station at the time.

One of the main ways we used to fight a fire was find a wide, dry creek bed or fire trail that ran across the front of the fire, well in advance of the fire front. Then, using the grader, we would make a parallel track about half a mile away from the creek or road. We would rest up during the heat of the day, keeping an eye out for wind changes and praying for a decent storm.

As soon as darkness fell we would be dropped off all along

the newly made track to burn back to the creek bed, burning the ground in between the two roads. We burnt back at night so we could see where the flames were and see if any of the fire had broken away behind us. The wind normally dropped at night, too, and the air had more moisture — or so we hoped!

The largest fire I ever fought was on Kamileroi Station. It involved the two mustering camps, the fencing and bore contractors and ringers from the adjoining station who had been sent over to help.

Our camp had been riding for two days to move the stock that was getting caught against holding paddock fences and hanging in hollows in front of the fire. Where we could we drove them to a gate but if the gate was too far away we would open the fences and drive them out of harm's way. It was great riding, like mad mustering, being able to canter back to where we had fresh horses and then back out again.

We had a huge camp set up to feed and bed down the men, well away from the fire. Not many got back to camp, they just stopped and slept in the shade whenever they could.

The burning back was an enormous job. The fire was burning on a very wide front and we had marked out a large plain as our last stand. We had been burning back for five days but, with the wind behind it, the fire kept on jumping our burnt-off areas.

So here we were in the middle of the plain. We could hear the fire and see it in the distance. The roos, emus and birds were heading out. They kept clear of us but the snakes and spiders were another worry. A group of us was sent on the old Blitz with the flamethrower to make a quick dash across the front of the fire about half a mile in front of it.

I was standing on the back of the Blitz next to the ringer with the flamethrower. We stopped and lit the flame and with that burning at full bore we took off across the face of the fire.

The heat and the roar of the fire and all the flying rubbish made it seem that we were driving into hell. We weren't on a road, so the Blitz was bouncing and swaying all over the place. As the flame from the thrower hit the grass the flames took off and with a roar started to race flat out as they were sucked into the face of the oncoming fire. We had only got about two miles across the front when the driver yelled that the fire was beating us and he was going to make a run for the break where the others were burning back.

We yelled for him to go. The main fire was huge and gaining on us at a great rate. We kept the thrower going out the back of the Blitz as the main fire jumped and flew across the plain. The burn back the others had started was coming up in front of us. As we hit this fire there were flames all around the Blitz. I had the top off the ship's tank and was throwing water over us to put the flying burning debris out and cool us off. When we broke through onto the burnt ground the heat was nearly overpowering. Then, as quickly as we came in, we were out the other side and on the fire trail with the other group of ringers shouting and waving.

No rest. There was a lot more work to do because the burn back they were attempting here was going to be too close to the road as it wasn't burning back towards the fire fast enough. This meant when the burn back and the fire met, the fire would jump the road.

'Back to the creek, we'll start another fire from there. Come on you bastards, shake a leg. Doc, you go in the ute to that patch of gidgee and burn back from the fire trail,' the head stockman yelled as he jumped into the Blitz and drove away.

We were black and very tired. I drove the station ute with Allen and Bill to the gidgee scrub.

'We had better step on it, the fire's nearly in the scrub,' Bill said as we came to a halt and piled out.

'Okay, we'll take these oily rags on poles off the road towards the fire and start our burn. Spread out, and as soon as I get my end burning I'll drive down and pick you up. I'll blow the horn for you to come out on to the road, okay?' I asked.

They both answered yes and headed off along the track with their burning brands.

I had been lighting the grass and fallen trees for some time and moving as fast as I could. I was feeling very tired and my eyes were stinging, so I stopped for a breather. It was nearly dawn. I looked around. My burning back fire was going well, too well. I didn't panic — I looked and listened.

The roar of the fire filled my ears. I don't know how I hadn't heard it before. Then it came to me. Of course, the wind had freshened. Now I could see the flames. They were racing towards me through the tops of the trees. I ran for the ute, started it and drove along the track, sounding the horn to attract the others' attention. Suddenly in front of me was a blackened figure staggering towards me out of the swirling smoke.

'The fire's going to go through here in the next few minutes, Doc. Let's get the hell out of here,' Bill croaked at me.

'We have to find Allen first. He should be on the track if he's heard the horn,' I yelled over the noise.

I drove along to where I could see Allen's burn back had ended.

'Come on, he should be here somewhere. You can see where the fire he's been setting is up to,' I said as we stopped. We jumped out and started to call to him. 'Hey, Allen, hurry up mate. That fire is racing towards us.'

I started to run around in the smoke looking for him, aware of the roar of the approaching fire. I rounded a fallen tree and fell over him! He was lying curled up fast asleep on the ground.

'Al, come on, wake up!' I leant down and yelled in his ear. 'Bill, give us a hand over here, I've found him.'

I started trying to pull Allen to his feet as Bill came running out of the smoke. Al was groggy.

'Want to sleep, leave me,' he mumbled and struggled to lie down.

'Shut up, you stupid bastard.'

We got him to his feet between us and started back in the direction of the ute. We weren't going to make it. The fire was all around us and the wet cloths we had wrapped around our faces were nearly dry, making it hard to breathe.

Whoosh! Bang!!!!!!

A huge ball of gas exploded around us, sending the ute up in flames.

'Christ, we're going to burn alive. What in the hell are we going to do?' Bill yelled as he stared through wild bloodshot eyes at the flames all around us. I looked around quickly.

'Our only chance is to try running through the fire and on to the burnt ground behind. Come on, let's go. It's our one and only chance.'

I didn't wait for an answer. I started to drag the two of them towards the flames. Suddenly the air was too hot to breathe and the heat was unbearable around us. We could hear the oily gas from the trees exploding and I think it was the fear of being caught in a fireball that made us move as fast as we did. Then we were through onto the burnt, searing hot ground. We had to keep moving. Our feet felt on fire and we couldn't see because of the smoke and flying cinders. We were nearly ready to give up, as the heat was making us dizzy.

Splash!! Water was hitting us in the face. We couldn't see it but we could hear the motor of the Blitz.

'Run, you bastards, run over here,' the head stockman and the other ringers yelled at us. The ringers in the truck, seeing the wind freshen, had come back looking for us, saw the ute go up and used the grader to cut a track through the fire. Then they'd raced across the burnt ground to get as close as possible to where they had last seen us. Everyone thought we had been caught by the fire and burnt to death when they couldn't find us. The men on the truck were amazed when we came stumbling out through the flames onto the burnt ground.

The ringers came running up, grabbed us and half-carried us to the truck, then poured water all over us to put out our smouldering clothes and cool us down. They threw us on board as the truck took off to get off the burnt ground before the tyres blew from the heat.

We were coughing and our eyes felt as if they were on fire. The truck was away from the fire and heat and heading to where the grader had made the road into an airstrip, a very rough one at that. They bundled us into a Cessna and after a bumpy take off (we were in safe hands — the pilot was an ex-fighter pilot from World War II) we flew into the station for treatment. We had blistered feet, singed hair, burnt hands and very bloodshot eyes.

We were sitting around, exhausted, in our quarters.

'Christ, we were lucky that wind was pushing the fire so fast, or we would never have made it through to the burnt ground,' Bill said. 'And you, you silly bastard, you wanted to sleep,' he said as he looked over at Allen — who was sound asleep on his bed.

What a Shirt of a Day

We were in camp up near the Myally–Lorraine station boundary. This muster was hard work because the cattle were wild and the country was rough, plus the boundary wasn't marked by any prominent features. We had a full camp with ringers from both properties helping with the muster so there was a lot of show-off riding and cutting out to try to prove who had the best horses.

Another point, and a good one, about this end of the property was the large packs of dingoes.

The manager, Jim Mitchell, had convinced the company that dingoes didn't travel around. They had their own areas where they bred and hunted, and he argued that if the company increased the station's bounty for dingo scalps, in about 18 months there wouldn't be many left. After a lot of humming and hawing, the company agreed to a 12-month trial period.

During this time dingoes shot on Kamileroi were worth about four pounds, which was a lot of money since my wage at the time was 12 pounds a week. We carried revolvers in our saddle bags and if we saw a pack of dingoes we would walk our horse as close as possible to the pack, then kick it into a gallop and ride down as many as we could. Riding them down meant that we rode up alongside the running dingo and let fly with our revolver.

The head stockman was not impressed and told us off if we galloped the horses around too much instead of mustering, so we took to carrying rifles so we could hit the dingoes without galloping our horses. We got away with carrying these arms because the manager wanted the scheme to work and the ringers were happy making more than their wages every month. It was one of the only times that I have seen ringers, on their day off, catch a horse and ride out hunting.

The manager proved his point because 12 months down the track you were flat out seeing a dingo on Kamileroi and any that you did see took off as soon as they heard or saw you coming.

We also had a bounty on wild pig snouts and tails. For a long while there was a good lurk in these snouts and tails until an old boundary rider was caught. What he and most of the mustering camp's ringers would do (I later found out it was common practice throughout the Gulf) was to put two holes in dried apricots with a leather punch to make them look like pig snouts. Placed out in the sun, they would go black and shrivelled — and believe me, they looked like the real thing. For years this boundary rider was the best pig shooter and poisoner in the area, until the day a pastoral inspector left a bag of collected snouts and tails out in a storm. A few days later, when he came to destroy them, he found they were covered in ants and the bags were filled with what looked and tasted like apricot jam. He never caught the people involved but the number of pig snouts collected went down.

While mustering the hills at this end of the station we were told by the management to keep an eye out for blacks who had wandered away from Doomadgee mission. During the time I was there we didn't see many, although we used to come across where they had been camped, because they would fade into the bush like ghosts whenever they heard the cattle and the horsemen coming. It wasn't hard to hear us coming, with whips cracking and the cattle bellowing.

The black ringers would often disappear at night and return in the morning. When I asked where they had been they would say that they had been visiting their family — women and children who were too afraid to go to the mission for fear of being split up. Usually we left them alone, although sometimes if they looked as if they were having a hard time, we would give them tea, flour and sugar. But we didn't make a habit out of it because it was against the law and we had to keep on the good side of the mission since we always hired our black workers there, except some of the old men who had been born on the station.

David Steel, a black ringer called Billy and I were mustering the north-western end of the station when two Myall blacks emerged from nowhere and approached us. Through the tracker they told us that an old rogue bull buffalo had trampled one of their shelters, nearly killing a baby. They had speared and tracked the wounded bull into prickly bush scrub only a few miles from where we were.

We had our rifles, so we asked them to show us where they had last seen it. We didn't go near buffalo when we were mustering. They would normally gallop off for some distance, then stand and watch us muster. Sometimes the odd buffalo would mix with the cattle we were mustering and then, as we tried to move the cattle with shouts and whips, they would come charging out of the mob at 100 miles an hour. Buffalo were always a bit of a worry.

But this time we weren't too worried. We thought the blacks only wanted us to kill the animal for food for them. We dismounted at the prickly bushes because the horses couldn't get through and they could smell the buffalo and were getting flighty.

'Billy, you show us the tracks. Doc and I will go in after him.'

Billy looked pleased to be hunting on foot. I was having second thoughts about the wisdom of walking into a prickly bush patch after a wounded buffalo. I took a sweaty hold of the rifle and slowly followed the two of them into the scrub.

Crash! Craaash! As we came past the first bushes the buffalo appeared, he was smashing his way through bushes as he thundered down on us. His horns looked as wide as the front of a jeep.

Bang! Bang! Bang!

David hit him with about three shots to the head but these only made him cranky. After he fired, David threw himself to one side under a large prickle bush. By some madness the tracker and I were caught together. Somehow the belt I wore with my pocket knife, watch and matches all in leather pouches had caught in Billy's clothes.

'This way, you idiot,' I yelled as I pulled towards the right. It seemed that Billy was as determined as me to get out of the way — but to the left. We were trying to get out of the charging buffalo's way in opposite directions, so our feet were moving but we were standing still.

Craaaaash! Through the prickly bushes — not round them — came this express train from hell.

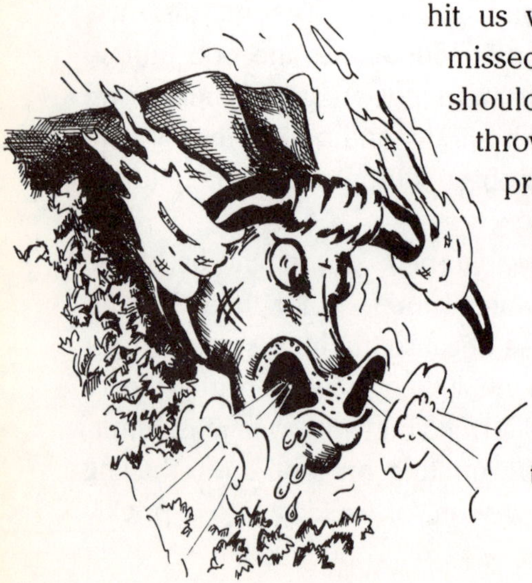

Riiiiippppppp! Teeeaaaar! Just before he hit us we came apart. The horns missed us but the massive shoulders slammed into us, throwing both of us into the prickly bushes on either side of the ton of rippling muscle. As I crashed into the branches I felt my shirt leave my back and the thorns rip into my bare skin. I crashed down under the prickly bush and scrambled around in the bulldust for my rifle, expecting to get a horn through me at any moment. I cocked the rifle as I spun around on one knee and saw the buffalo standing a few metres away, shaking his head with two shirts hanging off his horns.

David came running up.

'Shoot for the heart Doc, NOW!' David and I fired at the same time, aiming behind the shoulder.

The buffalo was charging towards us and as the shots hit him, he nosedived into the ground and slid to a halt at our feet. I think I took my first breath then.

'My bloody shirt is stuffed,' I said to David as I retrieved what was left of it off the beast's horns. I put it on to soak up some of the blood from the thorn scratches. John looked at Billy and me dripping blood and started going on about what a foolhardy thing to have done. If either of us had been hurt it was miles to the camp and even if we had made it back there we would have had to wait until the Flying Doctor was called and could find somewhere to land to pick us up. We always seemed to think about problems like this after we had done something foolish.

We sent one of the ringers back to the camp to get the butchering knives. Our pocketknives were no match for the tough hide. We butchered the beast, giving a lot to the blacks and their families that had materialised out of nowhere. We loaded some of the meat into bags and carried it back to the camp on our horses.

The cook was happy with the change of diet. He made us cut it into steaks, then beat the hell out of it. The meat tasted great but it was very chewy! We also minced it and the cook made good shepherd's pie and rissoles.

After a wash that night the scratches didn't seem so bad, they were just sore for a few days.

Riding an Angel

Out in the mustering camp, we had a new lot of horses brought in from being spelled, since the ones we had been using were stuffed and needed resting.

I had my own string of horses but we were all given some of the station horses to make up our string. We had around eight to ten horses for mustering and a couple for campdrafting.

One of the new ones I was given, after two ringers turned her down, was a small stock pony called Black Angel. John Steel, the head stockman, said, 'She's a good goer but be careful. She could buck a bit.'

The first time I caught her I ran my hands all over her. She was quiet and didn't seem to mind the attention. When I saddled her up and mounted her, instead of pigrooting, she was as good as gold. I galloped her around the yard while the other ringers were saddling their horses and then it was time to go. I was let out of the yard and this is when I expected her to buck but she was great and didn't put a foot wrong. I thought that John had only been kidding, the mare had a good mouth and a good gait. One of the ringers who had rejected her rode up.

'Be careful, the bitch is just waiting for a good time to put a few into you. She's not called the Black Angel for nothing, believe me.'

We had a long way to go out to muster, so we rode along slowly in the warm morning sun. I was trying not to daydream as I normally did because I thought that the ringer might possibly be right about the Black Angel. Nothing happened. She was the perfect stock horse all morning while we mustered into a waterhole about 12 miles from the camp and the yards.

By lunchtime we were holding around 1600 head, nearly all the cattle from that area. We had them resting in the shade of the white box trees around the waterhole. John was sending us in threes to boil our quart pots for tea and have a quick sit in the shade while we bolted our lunch down. The others stayed out to hold the cattle.

The normal practice whenever we came into a dinner camp was to dismount and loosen the saddle girths to make our horses comfortable, then take our pots down to the waterhole, fill them with water, and put them on the fire to make our tea. Next we'd sit in the shade and eat our two slabs of damper, one end with corned beef and pickle and the other with plum or melon and lemon jam.

I had squatted down with the other two ringers to eat my lunch when John cantered over to tell us that the cattle on the west side were heading out from the dinner camp. We were needed to help head them off.

I jumped to my feet and ran down to the mare, untied her and swung aboard.

'Look out, Doc, your girth is loose,' John yelled as a warning.

As if on cue Black Angel flew into the air, twisting and bucking, I was sticking with her and she was going for it. I threw my glasses away.

'Yaaaahhhhooooo!' I yelled at the top of my voice. I wasn't too worried about the loose saddle, since I had my legs clamped to her sides. I had one hand in the air for balance but she was really trying to toss me off her back and she wasn't playing. She threw herself up into the air with her head down between her front legs.

Oh f . . . . . k!

I felt the saddle start to go forward over her withers and there was nothing I could do to save myself. The saddle had picked up speed and the mare felt it going, so she shot backwards. The ground came up to meet me as I came down face first into the bulldust.

'Don't let go of the reins or you'll be walking home, Doc,' I heard someone shout as I was pulled, saddle and all, across the ground. The saddle got hung up and I could feel the rein burning my hand as red hide ran across my palm and then was gone.

As the dust cleared I found myself left with the saddle still between my legs and my body spreadeagled in the bulldust. I was spitting dust and swearing while trying to see through the red haze without my glasses. The saddle girth was still done up, she had thrown me saddle and all.

The mare was off with her head held high so the reins wouldn't touch the ground, the cunning bitch! A couple of ringers tried to stop her but she was galloping down the side of the cattle. This spooked the cattle and they started to run in every direction as they tried to get away.

The head stockman rode up yelling to the ringers who were trying to catch the mare, 'Hey, don't worry about the bitch. Stop the f . . . ing cattle from spreading out and going bush.'

He turned in his saddle and said to me, 'You'll have to walk until you get to the holding paddock gate where the horse tailer's waiting for us with the fresh horses we're going to use to yard up. Your mare should be there too, if that brumby stallion doesn't see her.'

'Oh no, that bitch will pay for this.'

This wasn't all I said as I turned and picked up my saddle and blanket and started to walk towards the holding paddock gate, which was around eight miles away. I was walking behind the cattle feeling sorry for myself. I was hot, covered in dust and flies, with a saddle on my shoulder which felt like a ton weight, plus high Cuban-heeled riding boots which weren't good for walking long distances. Adding to my misery were the boys who were riding in the dust, pushing the mob along. They were laughing and making a great joke out of my plight. Strangely enough, I couldn't see the funny side.

After four miles I was feeling stuffed and wondering why I was doing this — there had to be an easier way to make a quid, when one of the boys yelled, 'Truck coming.'

I was so relieved. It was the cook in the Blitz. He told me as I climbed aboard that when my mare had turned up at the holding paddock gate the horse tailer had galloped back to the camp and got the cook to drive out in case I had been hurt.

The head stockman rode up and told me as soon as I got back that I was to saddle up the mare and ride her because he didn't want her to think she'd had a victory. I said, 'Okay.'

I wasn't looking forward to riding her because I thought she would try bucking again and she might get the better of me and throw me, loose saddle or not. I was very pleased to be aboard the Blitz and get a lift to the holding paddock gate. As we approached I could see my mare was tied up with the other horses.

'You'll have to be more careful with that one, she's a crafty little bitch,' the horse tailer said as I was saddling up.

'I know. She waits for you to relax, then sticks it into you.'

I put a crupper on her so the saddle wouldn't go over her head if she started to buck, pulled the surcingle as tight as I could, then led her around and tightened it again.

There was no horse yard for me to ride in, so I walked her out into the open away from the fence, pulled the near side rein up tight and grabbed a handful of mane, put my foot in the stirrup, put my knee into her shoulder and swung aboard — or that's what I thought I was going to do!

As I was halfway into the saddle she started to buck forward but the tight rein pulled her around. I landed up on the back of the saddle and, using the jug handle, I pulled myself back in. I couldn't find the stirrup because by this time we were airborne. This time I had her, or so I thought, so I stuck my heels in and let go of the jug handle.

Yaaaahoooo!

'Stick with her, Doc. You've got her!' The horse tailer was yelling encouragement to me.

One minute I was in control, the next I was in the air as she shot back under me. I think I hovered above the saddle while she bucked twice and then I was all over her from the withers to the rump. Somehow I stayed on and as suddenly as she had started she stopped.

'Hey, that was some ride. You're one of the few around who have stayed with her.'

Feeling proud of myself I rode her out to meet the other ringers to help drive the cattle into the holding paddock. In the morning we were going to campdraft the strangers and the cows and calves out before yarding.

I got to like the little mare after a while and rode her a lot. It didn't take long to know when she was getting up to something. She didn't have a bad bone in her body, she just liked to play around a bit. Most of the time she was good for me to show off on as she would buck high but straight ahead.

OP Rum, the Drink of Courage

The Cloncurry Rodeo was coming up and we were all going to town, so we were all in our quarters polishing boots, getting gear ready and all talking about the rides, the grog and the girls. I was more excited than the rest of the blokes as it was the first rodeo that I would be riding in. Everyone was giving me advice, since I was to ride a steer that was notorious. They told me about what would happen in the crush before the gate opened, how to put my hand under the girth rope and how it would be pulled down by a couple of ringers, then passed through my hand and then wound around my wrist. This made me feel very uneasy!

The light plane from the 'Curry flew over and I could hear them yelling to the ringers about meeting them in town that night. They were going to be there in around an hour and a half. We were travelling in the ute and the truck which would take many hours to get to the 'Curry. If all our vehicles were full it wouldn't be hard to get a lift, as the road was busy with at least three or four vehicles passing by an hour.

'Make sure that you do your swag up tight, Doc. With all the mob on the road it's going to be dusty.' I nodded in agreement, finished strapping up my swag and went out to see the light plane take off. There was another one circling to land and the whole place was buzzing with activity.

Next there was a lot of shouting out the front of the station store. 'The truck goes in five minutes, if you're not on it then you stay here,' the driver was yelling, sounding the horn and revving the engine.

We all piled on the back and got comfortable for the long journey. It normally took a day, including stops. Our first stop was Kajabbi for some beer, then on to Quamby for a few more, then the 'Curry. We were all booked into the snake pit at the back of the Oasis Hotel, as all the rooms in all the hotels were full. On the way in we had to stop a few times to pick up some of the ringers who had fallen off into the bulldust. I think the heat, plus warm beer and being covered in bulldust tends to upset your balance.

We arrived in the 'Curry late in the afternoon and headed straight for the bar. We had been warned by the managers not to get into fights about whose station or mustering camp was the best. Except at rodeo time, most of the larger stations would try not to let their mustering camps come to town when there was another station in town.

The town was bursting at the seams and everyone was drinking and talking at a million miles an hour. The town seemed to have a larger population of girls all of a sudden, so every now and then someone would get hit for swearing in front of the ladies.

That night John and I went with two of these ladies to the sideshows.

Some of these shows were tents with seats surrounding a high steel-framed ring where the spruiker was betting 100 pounds that no-one could ride the horses or

Brahmin bulls they would bring out and lead around. They looked placid and as if butter wouldn't melt in their mouths.

I was pretty drunk and so was John. We were showing off to the girls, saying that we could ride anything. The horse that was being led around the ring was the same size and velvet black colour as the one I rode at Kamileroi, Black Angel, so I thought, 'I can ride that'.

'Go on, show us,' they were shouting at us, so in the end John and I went around the back to the blokes running the show. They had heard the girls and some of the other ringers standing around yelling out for us to have a go.

'What are the rules?' John asked as they dropped him down bareback onto a piebald wild-eyed gelding.

'None. To win the money you have to be on his back when the bell rings. That's only one minute. Think you can do it?' the tent worker asked as he pulled the flank rope tight.

'Don't forget to take a picture, Doc,' John said to me, since he had given me his camera.

Before I could answer they had opened the gate. The horse bucked straight up into the air. As he bucked out into the small ring he was flying. I thought, 'Oh no, he's going to go straight through the rails on the other side.'

John let out a strangled yell as the horse came back underneath him and he started to fly towards the pipe rails. 'Shit, the camera.' I was still holding it but everything had happened so quickly I hadn't used it. I brought it up and took a picture of John spread-eagled on the rails on the other side. He hadn't hurt himself and the horse was standing in the centre of the ring as quiet as a lamb because the flank rope had been removed. John staggered over.

'It's your turn and I want to see you ride that little black mare. Did you get a photo?'

'Yes,' I said. 'It shows you in full flight.'

It took them a little time to get the black mare into the crush and I was sober and sweating by that time. I climbed down onto her back, grabbed hold of the handle and wrapped my legs around her.

One of the blokes helping leant over to me.

'She'll come out high, then when she comes down she'll twist to the left and then launch herself into the air.'

I nodded my thanks and thought, 'What's he talking about?'.

'Ready?'

I nodded agreement.

'Go!'

The mare shot out of that chute like a bullet. I think she pulled my arm out of its socket, then she was up — I thought that we were going through the canvas top of the tent. Coming down, I tried to remember what advice the bloke had told me.

It didn't matter. As she hit the ground she twisted and leapt back into the air. I felt my hand come free and my body was thrown up and out. The next thing I knew I was balancing on the top rail of the ring looking down on the seats and the people I was about to fall on.

Craaaaaashhh!

I hit the seating and lay there for a second or two, then tried to jump to my feet. I didn't make it as my head was spinning and the adrenaline was still pumping through my body. John and the girls came over and we made our way like a couple of cripples back to the pub lounge. I made my excuses early as some of us had been asked to help bring the rodeo horses in from the common.

A Prickly Situation

This was a sight. The unbroken horses were brought down the main street and wheeled into the showground. There were ringers and townspeople out in the street to turn the horses and everyone else was there to see if any of the horses would go through the shop windows. It was a mad 20 minutes or so — ringers yelling and horsemen trying to stop the horses from breaking back. After some liquid lunch I hobbled over to the rodeo because I was still sore and stiff from the ride and fall the night before.

John met me near the chutes.

'I've put you down for the bullock ride, so don't go away.'

'Oh no, I can't ride. I feel like shit.'

'You have to, the whole camp is betting on your ride.'

'I haven't got the gear,' I said, hoping that would put them off, but no, someone lent me his bullock rope and another bloke his chaps. I had brought my roping gloves, so there was nothing I could say. I hung around watching the different events leading up to mine. I was hoping all the bullocks had escaped and as time wore on I was feeling terrible.

Then it was my turn. As I climbed up onto the top rail of the crush, a loud cheer went up from the ringers who were backing me. I didn't like their chances of winning.

'Come on, we haven't got all day, get down on his back,' the chute handler said as he pulled my arm. I looked down at the large hairy brown back — the animal looked huge. I slid my legs down either side of him and, as he snorted and jumped around, I could feel the sides of the chute pushing against my legs.

'Give us your right hand,' the handler said, 'and put it on here,' pointing at the bullock's withers. I placed my hand there with my palm up and he placed the girth rope over my palm and started to pull it tight. I was committed, my hand was now trapped between the rope and the bullock's hide. When they got it tight enough they brought the end of the rope back and I closed my hand on it. I remembered what the ringers had shown me at camp — to pull myself forward so that the arm holding the rope came over the top of my leg. Then I had to press down with all my force on that leg.

Christ, there was so much to remember.

'Don't forget, the more you rake him with your spurs, the more points you get. You okay?'

I can't remember if I answered him. The bell rang and the gate of the chute opened. At first the bullock didn't seem to want to go anywhere, he just stood there.

'Hook him, make the bastard go.'

I took that advice and for good measure let out a yell. Yahooo!!!!! I wished I hadn't.

The bullock swung out of the chute with a snort and went straight up in the air. I was trying to get it right. Hook when you are going up and grip when you hit the ground. I was going well, I could feel the skin moving under me. We hit the ground and came up into the air. I was a little to one side and the bullock could feel it, the next minute I was on his side, then his rump. I was being thrown around like a rag doll. The only thing staying in one place was my right hand because the rope had it firmly anchored. I felt there were times I was doing handstands on this animal's back. I opened my hand and the sheer force of the next buck wrenched it free and sent me cartwheeling through the air to land in a heap on the ground a few yards from the chute. I felt as if I had travelled around the showground in the few seconds I had been aboard. One of the clowns came and helped me up and I staggered over to the chutes.

'Did you get a photo, John?' I asked him.

'Yeah, Doc. Hey, don't go away. I've put your name down for the bareback rides after the bullock rides are finished.' He had a smile on his face, which grew bigger when he saw the look on mine. I think if the pounding head, the dry mouth and the soreness from the last fall had let me, I would have punched him out.

'Here, take a mouthful of this.' He thrust a beer bottle into my hand. I put it up to my mouth and took a long swig.

Ppppaaah!

Christ, it was OP house rum. I stood there gagging, with eyes watering but once it was down for good I started to feel better.

We hung around the back of the chutes helping and trying to keep busy until the time came to draw the horses we were to ride from the hat.

I drew a grey clumper that looked mean and was called the Doctor as most people that rode him needed one. That made me feel wonderful, if I didn't have the DTs before that I did now. I sat in frozen horror on the rails watching the rides before me. They were all good horses and they got rid of their riders quickly.

One rider came up to me. 'You've picked a top horse with that one, you could win if you ride him.'

'Thanks.' I was nearly going to tell him he could ride him himself.

Then came the moment that I had been dreading.

'Ladies and gentlemen, here's a good double, a ringer called Doc riding one of the best — the Doctor.'

'When the whip cracks we'll come up either side. Which side do you prefer, Doc?' the riders who were hazing had come up to the chute gates to ask me. I lifted my right hand.

'Okay, right side it is. Best of luck, mate.'

I lowered myself down on to the horse's back in the chute, asking for help as the horse was jumping around and banging my legs on both sides of the chute.

'The easiest way to fix that is to let you out. Are you ready, Doc?' the handler asked me. I nodded and saw his hand go up to signal the chute was opening to the time keepers.

The chute gate was flung open and the horse swung to get out. I had a good hold of his head with the rope halter.

'Go, Doc, start hooking,' the cry went up. 'Hook him.'

I came out of the chute sitting comfortable and hooking like hell but the grey horse was an old hand. He galloped towards the centre of the showground, throwing a few small pigroots but once he had some speed up he became fair dinkum. He dropped his head down as far as he could between his front legs and headed for the sky. On this buck he climbed up so high I could see out over the showground's boundary fence — not that I had time for too much looking around. We were coming down to the ground again and I had to work out which way he was going to go. He hit the ground with a bone-crushing jar and I saw him swing his head — we were going off to the right. Up we went again. I had picked it right, as we were going up I realised if he kept bucking in this direction we were going to hit the fence. I tried to pull on the halter to turn his head but that only made it worse, he threw his head up and galloped straight for the fence.

'Don't do it, you stupid bastard,' I yelled in his ear. I could hear the riders galloping down behind us to try and turn the Doctor away from the fence but they weren't going to make it. The scene in front of me was chaos. People had been picnicking with the food spread out on the bonnets of their cars which faced the fence. But now, instead of a quiet picnic scene, families were scattering in every direction. It was too late for me to do anything, we lifted into the air again and cleared the single rail fence.

Craasssh!

We came down on the bonnet of a car. Food went everywhere and I held on for grim life. I didn't want to fall off in case the horse came down on top of me jamming me between the parked cars. As the bonnet collapsed under our combined weight the horse leapt over the top of the car to the ground and started to buck in the direction in which the largest group of people were running. I was now looking for a chance to leave him but at the same time I had a handful of mane and I was gripping with my legs. The crowd parted as we came up to them. Then we were through the running people.

'Oh bloody hell!' I yelled as we headed straight under some tall prickly bushes. The horse started to buck up into the branches, he really wanted to get rid of me now and, of course, I was on top so I was being driven up in amongst the bloody sharp prickles. As the horse dropped back to the ground I was dragged back down through the prickles. Every time I went up or down I left skin and pieces of my shirt on the thorns. I was swearing at the top of my voice as I lost count of how many times I was pushed up the tree. Suddenly the horse got rid of me. He went up and came down but this time he left me caught up in the prickly branches. He galloped off, leaving me with only my feet showing. They had to back a truck under the tree and, by standing on the tray, they were able to cut me down. I wasn't badly hurt, just a lot of bleeding scratches, but I looked bad when they drove out from underneath.

The nurse and doctor patched me up and after a few mouthfuls of OP I was stiff and sore for only a short time. But the next morning, when I tried to roll out of my swag, I found that I couldn't stand up.

I Meet an Old Friend

Years later I was working as head cataloguer for Foyles bookshop in London. I had my own office on the third floor. I originally joined them as an assistant accountant because I found in the early sixties you could tell your employers any story about your job experiences if you were a mad colonial boy in London with nothing to lose. It was easy to get work because we were the flavour of the year.

I told Foyles I had done a librarian's course at Sydney University and two years accountancy (if you can class bookkeeping at school and bookkeeping by correspondence as accountancy).

So here was I, the bull from the bush, working with all these people who hadn't seen any open spaces bigger than a park. At lunchtime and after work I used to go to the local pub called the Pillars of Hercules which was nearly next door to the bookshop. There I used to tell bush stories for beers and, if I was lucky, a ploughman's lunch. Everyone drank pints of this warm beer called Watneys. I found that after a while you grew to like it.

Let me set the scene at the pub.

It was an old pub in Soho. The interior was lined with old dark timber panels and large ceiling beams and the bar was a huge wooden affair which ran the length of the room, with old porcelain beer taps and glasses hanging above it. Behind was a big mirrored sideboard affair, with spirit bottles on shelves and mountains of food spread out on the sideboard under it.

The food looked great — smoked salmon from Scotland, rare roast beef, leg ham on a porcelain stand, cheeses from all over England, salads and crisp bread rolls. It used to make my mouth water since I could only afford to eat if someone liked my stories and was ordering lunch. The pub was always pretty packed but the group I was telling stories to would form a circle around me so I had room. I needed room because I would tell bush stories with lots of hand movements and sounds, using actions like whipping off an imaginary hat and hitting the imaginary horse I was riding on.

Here I was, thousands of miles from the Gulf, jumping around in a circle of excited Poms. These people had never seen or heard about the outback, or anything about the people that live and work there. And they had never seen anything like me either. I would make the noise of the whips cracking and the cattle rushing and farting noises for bucking horses trying to get rid of me, and beers would get spilt as I got caught up in the telling. By the time a session finished I would be standing in a pool of spilt beer, half-drunk but happy.

One Friday night I was in full swing. It was pay day, everyone was buying me beers and the stories were getting wilder since I could see I had the crowd eating out of my hand. I was knocking over lots of beer and showering everyone with it. It was near the end of the evening. I had just ridden another wild horse and the audience was thinning out as they headed for the tube station and home.

The barman called to me and handed me a glass of spirits. I sniffed, it was my favourite drink — rum.

'The gentleman down the bar asked me to give you this, with his compliments,' the barman said as he nodded towards a bloke who was sitting on his own down the bar.

I raised the glass to acknowledge him — and did a double take. The bloke was wearing a ringer's hat. He was as brown as a berry and had a grin from ear to ear. Then I recognised him. I pushed through the crowd, yelling, 'Tom, you bastard. What in the hell are you doing here?'

The last time I had seen Tom was on Kamileroi Station in the Gulf about four years earlier. He jumped up from his stool and I threw the rum down and got rid of the glass as I made my way to greet him. I was so excited to see someone from home we came together like two prize fighters, arms everywhere.

All the questions came out on top of each other. 'What are you doing here?' 'How long are you here for?' 'Why didn't you come up and say hello instead of sitting here?'

'Slow down, Doc. You always did talk too fast and too much,' Tom said in his slow Queensland drawl. 'I sat down here so I could listen to your bull. Your riding seems to have got better since you've been in England. Wait 'til I get back to the blokes in the Gulf and tell them you're riding all their horses.'

He sat down and laughed. 'I didn't want to interrupt you while you were telling your stories, seeing me might have stopped you telling them. Anyway, you were in the middle of one of my rides and I didn't know I could ride so well.'

We sat around until the pub closed. Then we went to his hotel for more drinking and talking. Seeing someone from the Gulf was just great, I caught up on all the happenings around a mob of stations.

Tom had been in London for a few days, he was sailing the next day for the States. This was his big trip.

'I thought instead of blowing all my money in the pub or going down to Brisbane to live it up, I'd go around the world and see how other people lived. When I get back I'll be a manager and too busy to travel,' Tom said to me. 'It was only luck that made me come into that hotel tonight — and what a surprise to see you holding forth. Keep the stories rolling. The ringers will be pleased to know their exploits are known as far as the Old Dart.'

In the weeks that followed, when a story was getting a little bit exaggerated I would look down the bar, to see if Tom was there listening.

Appendices

About the Properties

The Australian Estates properties I worked on were all part of a breeding and fattening set-up that expanded throughout Queensland, from the breeding and bullock depots in the Gulf to Mt Howard, west of Brisbane, where the best store cattle were fattened for the Brisbane market.

Dalgonally Station

Situated north-west of Julia Creek, the property was around 600 square miles and fenced with bore drains supplying water to the paddocks. The country was flat, black soil plains with dry channels and rose up to hills on the western side. The property was used as a depot to take the cattle from the breeding stations further north and make up uniform mobs. The older bullocks and spade cows went to Townsville, the best store cattle went on a long droving trip to south Queensland to be fattened.

Granada Station

Situated north of Quamby, the property was around 200 square miles, fenced, mainly flat, scrubby country with some good black soil plains. This property was a herd bull stud producing shorthorn bulls and, while I was there, they had Zebu and Santa

Gertrudis, and started a great line of Drought Masters. These bulls were sent to all Australian Estates properties and there was a public sale once a year. One year we mustered and, after drafting, had, in one mob, 2000 two- to three-year-old bulls.

Kamileroi Station

Situated north of Dobbyn, the property was around 2000 square miles, unfenced and was a mixture of plains, river country and hills to the west. It was a breeding station with 27 000 head of breeders — the bang tail muster when I was there. There were over 400 horses, not counting the brumbies.

Lists of Equipment

Loading the Truck for Mustering

Bush radio and batteries
Canvas flies (tarpaulins)
Cook's tent and fold-up beds
Spare gear — saddles, rope halters, bridles, leather for repairs and pack saddles
Hobbles and bells
Crowbars, axes, post hole shovels, number eight wire and tie wire, iron standards, driver and pliers, Donaldson wire strainers
2 drums of carbide and carbide lights
Candles, both bought and camp made (we made these from boiled down fat put into old jam tins)
Fuel in 44-gallon drums
Water in 44-gallon drums
Buckets, since we had to cart water for the cook
2 boxes of tools for truck and windmill repairs (this included pulleys and block and tackles)

2 boxes of assorted nuts and bolts
Ropes
Chains
Branding irons and earmarking pliers
Stockholm tar and other first-aid gear for horses
Horseshoes and shoeing gear
A ship's tank for getting water from bores and turkey nests
A long rubber hose
A first-aid box (with very little in it, just bandages, Aspro, Dettol, cotton wool, sticking plaster and insect cream for bites)
Firefighting gear — bags, rakes, beaters on handles, a flamethrower with a tin of petrol and some backpack sprays.

Equipment for the Cook

Camp ovens, pans, cooking tripod, hooks and cooking utensils
Butchers' knives and steels
Vegetables, canned
Fruit, canned
Jam
Chutney (the yellow kind)
Curry powder
Mixed herbs
Worcestershire sauce
Tomato sauce
Kraft processed cheese
Powered eggs, large four gallon drums of it
Potatoes, fresh and powdered
Dried mixed vegetables
Carrots
Tea
Flour
Sugar
Lemon essence

Vanilla essence
Yeast
Baking powder
Gravox
Tinned butter (which came in round tins and always separated)
Tinned powdered milk
Wax matches (Vespas)
Plates, spoons, knives and forks
Metal hanging fly safes (to hang meat and sweet food away from ants and flies)

Personal gear

One canvas swag with the following:

Something to read (I belonged to Foyles book club in London, so I got four books a month)
A diary and writing gear (for me it was my bookkeeping correspondence course)
Clothes, socks, pants, shirts, underpants and a leather belt for your trousers
A leather belt for carrying a watch, two cutting knives, a pocketknife and a tin of wax matches, all in leather pouches
Soap, razor and toothbrush
Tobacco and tobacco paper
Cordial (most of the bore water was so bitter you could only drink it with cordial)
Mosquito net (a green rectangular net with material strips on top so that you could tie each of the four corners to sticks stuck in the ground, and material around the edges so that you could tuck it under the edges of your swag)
Any handicraft you were doing, like plaiting, leather embossing or making bridles and whips
Spurs

Two pairs of riding boots
Leggings
Stockwhip
Saddle with quart pot and saddlebag
Bridle
Fly veils (flies out there were as thick as dust)
Saddle cloths
A rifle and ammo
Leather chaps (in case we were mustering in prickly bush or grass seed country)
A catching rope

Setting up Camp

The head stockman drove the vehicle with the cook up front and two jackaroos and two ringers on top of the load.

We would get out before the others, cut branches for the bower shed and table, chop firewood and cart water, set up the cook's tent and his cooking area, check the horse yards and walk the boundary of the night horse paddock with wire, strainer and pliers.

The rest of the camp would ride out with the horses, normally arriving in the afternoon. When they arrived the head stockman would send out four ringers, two in each direction, along the horse paddock fences to check them before we let the horses go.

Glossary

Artesian bore A hole bored into the earth to find water and pipe it to the surface

Banker A flooding river which has overflown its banks

Blacks Australian Aborigines

Blacks' camp An area near the station or town set aside for Aborigines to live

Blitz truck A World War II four-wheel drive truck

Bolter A horse that gets the bit between its teeth and takes off

Boundary rider A person who lives alone and checks the fences and bores

Bulldogging Roping and tying an animal (from a horse)

Bulldust Very fine dust, like talcum powder

Camp draft Holding cattle in a mob and drafting out the cows with calves before yarding

Cattle duffers People who steal cattle

Channel Country The Gulf area of Queensland where all the rivers and channels run into the sea

Cowboy A person who works around the homestead, milking, gardening, etc

Cracker Three or four inches of plaited horse hair or cotton fixed to the end of a whip to make it crack

Crupper A strap fitted to the back of the saddle which goes round the tail

Cutting out Taking cattle out of the mob without a yard, to keep the cows with their calves

Cutting-out horse Special top horses used to bring the cattle out of the mob

Drafting Separating the cattle by size or age group

Drafting yards Small yards used to separate the different sizes and age groups of cattle

Face The front of a mob of cattle

Fettler Railway line worker

Fly A piece of canvas used as a cover

Gidgee scrub A type of Australian tree that grows in clumps

Gulf Country Area around the Gulf of Carpentaria

Head stockman The stockman who runs the mustering camps

Hobbles Two straps with a chain and swivel fixed to the horse's front legs to stop the horse running away

Horse breaker A man who trains a horse in three days to take a rider

Horse tailer The ringer in charge of the horses

Jackaroo An apprentice stockman or manager (usually from a middle-class background)

Kangaroo Valley An area of London where most Australians lived

Killers Cattle set aside for killing on the station for meat

Landrover A four-wheel drive jeep with a canvas top

Mob A large herd of cattle

Monkey A strap fitted to the saddle to assist in mounting and riding rough horses

Mustering To round the cattle up and drive them to a yard or new paddock

On the wing Riding at the side of a mob to stop them getting away

Pigroot Bucking forward and kicking up. Most mornings fresh horses would pigroot

Poddy dodging Stealing young unbranded or ear marked calves and putting your own brand on them

Recanterline To replace the horsehair stuffing of a saddle

Ringer An Australian stockman

R M Williams Maker and supplier of the best gear for ringers

Ship's tank A square water tank made of iron and

use, with high knee pads and back

Stockman A man who looks after cattle

Strangers Other stations' cattle

Striker A horse that lifts its front hooves and throws them out and down

String of horses The horses that are given to a stockman to do his work, normally around ten to 12 head

Surcingle A strap that fits over the saddle and holds it in place

Swag A rectangle of canvas that a ringer keeps all his gear in and sleeps on

Temperance Hotel Non-alcoholic hotel

The wet The rainy season — from November to February

Turkey nest An earth mound hollowed out to hold the water from a bore

Up the duff Pregnant

Willeys A four-wheel drive ute

Wing of a yard A fence running out from the gate of a yard to help when yarding